DO IT!
F***ING DO IT!

Scenes from an actor's life

Stuart McGugan

WETSOCKS BOOKS

ALSO FROM WETSOCKS BOOKS

Non-fiction

YOUR CAPTAIN SPEAKING
Views from the flight deck

Captain Scott Birrell

WALKING THE LINE
Two oldies (and one dodgy hip) tackle the entire Western Front

Nick and Fiona Jenkins

LETTERS TO 281

Alan Jenkins

Fiction

DEATH & TAXES
(and other uncertainties)

Fergus Linnane

THE PALE PARABOLA
(and other stories)

Fergus Linnane

Jim McGugan, manoeuvring his way very carefully down the many steps from the Royal Mile to Princess Street during the busy Edinburgh Festival:

"THANK GOD FOR BANISTERS!"

Edinburgh 2023

Published by Wetsocks Books,
Hebden Bridge, West Yorkshire

Illustrated by Ian Kinnear

Ian is a landscape painter who lives and works on the east coast of Scotland.
"Illustrating Stuart's stories has been a diverting departure from my painting and a return to a partnership enjoyed during our schooldays."

ISBN: 978-1-8384417-3-9

CONTENTS

For Cordelia
and Mitch

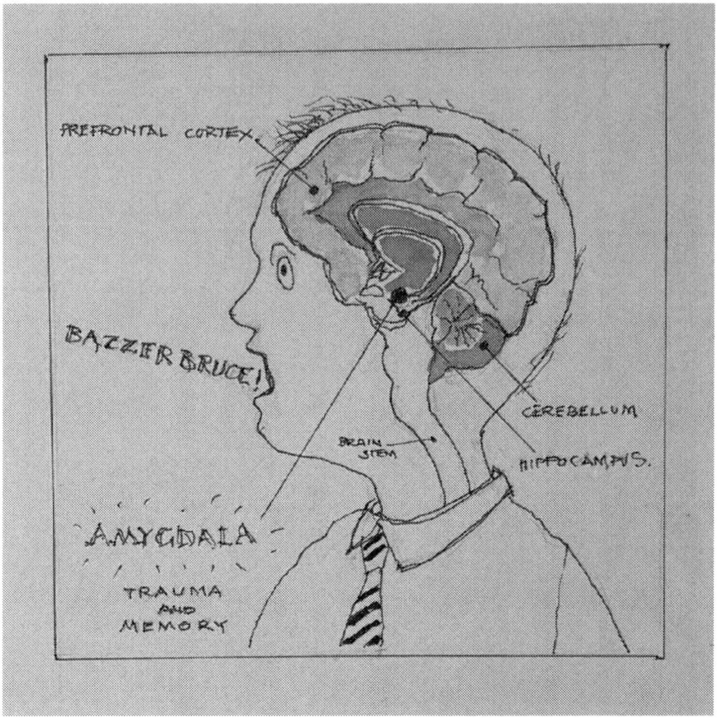
PREFRONTAL CORTEX
BAZZER BRUCE!
CEREBELLUM
BRAIN STEM
HIPPOCAMPUS.
AMYGDALA
TRAUMA AND MEMORY

BAZZER BRUCE

Researchers have long maintained that early undiagnosed trauma can blight and damage a growing child's adult wellbeing and happiness. Some forgotten or suppressed childhood incident can bedevil mature mental development. It can inform and guide choices and influence decisions, it can lead you astray, often unknowingly. Anyway, that's my story, and I'm sticking to it....

I think I know who to blame for any deep-rooted psychological upset in my childhood:

Bazzer Bruce.

I couldn't have been more than eight or nine, and there was a witness: my friend and fellow mischief-maker Wilson Ree. All this happened years ago, but in my memory it is as vivid as if it were only yesterday.

Wilson Ree and I were in Letham, casually strolling up the incline between Eck Low's ice cream shop – "best ice cream in Angus!" – and the Haven, the house of our mate Ed Valentine. Coming towards us, at speed, was Bazzer. He looked like he was probably hoping to catch the bus to Forfar. Nothing unusual in that.

I remember him as middle-aged, but I was eight or nine. Anyone over fifteen, to me, was middle-aged. And he was not a slim man, and that's why the sight of him running was intriguing to us both. He didn't change pace as he approached us downhill. We moved slightly to our right to allow him to pass.

There was no greeting. No "Aye lads! Whit dae ye think o' this?". In complete silence, it happened. In one unbroken, almost choreographed movement, Bazzer leapt high in the air, and simultaneously, resoundingly, cacophonously, farted. It lasted from take-off to landing. He didn't change step, he didn't say anything, just continued on his way, leaving two stunned wee boys in his wake.

"Eh? What was that?" said Wilson. "Ah don't know," I said.

He was a grown-up, for goodness sake! What's goin' on here? If anyone grown-up can arbitrarily defy the natural order of things, what could we kids rely on, have faith in?

What did that dramatic moment of bizarre adult behaviour unleash in the unconsciousness of the eight-year-old me? Serious psychological trauma, perhaps. That moment of anarchy, suppressed, unacknowledged, could have tainted or influenced my behaviour for subsequent decades.

It might explain a few things. Why did I, only a few years later, from the most improbable background, announce that I wanted to be an actor? Why, when that was blocked, did I choose to be a newspaperman? Why, even then, was the need to act irresistible?

Could it explain the enthusiasm for alcohol?

Or the countless thoughtless deeds in adolescence, continuing into adulthood?

Why do I still, in spite of the annual disappointment,

continue to support Forfar Athletic? Could it possibly be that had it not been for Mr Bruce's airborne flatulence all those years ago, none of the above, or the following, would ever have happened?

Enjoy…

Letham, Angus, Scotland, 1952.

ARTHUR BINNIE AND THE KAMA SUTRA

Saturday lunchtime at the *Aberdeen Evening Express* was a relaxing time. A couple of early editions – mostly a rehash of the morning sister paper, the *Press and Journal,* with any breaking Saturday morning news – had gone to bed, and we had all been to the pub for lunch. Time to tidy up and prepare for the Sporting Green.

Most major towns in the 1960s had a morning and an evening paper. The Aberdeen paper, the *Press and Journal,* had gained notoriety with its parochialness years before, with its headline on the sinking of the Titanic:

"Aberdeen Man Feared Lost At Sea."

With the *Evening Express* on Saturday afternoon, there was a race to get an edition with all the sporting results out on to the streets to catch the late shoppers and sports fans, either in the pub or on their way home. The distinctive green-tinted paper contained a full report of the exploits of the Aberdeen team – the Dons – and all senior Scottish League football matches, plus a nod in the direction of the top English teams, especially those run by Scottish managers. Our job in the sub-editors department was to get the thing out and into the delivery vans as quickly as possible. Each sub had a handful of reports – usually seriously over-written, as the reporters were paid by the published line – to précis, put a headline on, and fit into the space allotted by the chief sub-editor, Arthur Binnie.

Arthur came from Arbroath, thirty miles south of Aberdeen, and was a journalistic legend even before he joined the *Evening Express*, thanks to the most audacious political "robbery" in postwar Britain. On Christmas Day 1950, four Glasgow University students removed the Stone of Destiny from its resting place under the Coronation Chair in Westminster Abbey, and took it back to Scotland. The stone, on which all Scottish kings were crowned, had initially been "re-located" as spoils of war from Scone in Perthshire to Westminster Abbey in London by England's Edward I in 1296, and the students, all supporters of Home Rule for Scotland, believed they were simply returning stolen property to its original home.

In 1952, Arthur Binnie was a reporter on the Arbroath weekly paper when, through local contacts and shrewd professionalism, he learned that the stone was going to be returned, eventually, to the nation by being placed on the high altar in Arbroath Abbey. It was a fitting homecoming, because in 1320, the Scottish Declaration of Independence was unveiled in the abbey. It was a reporter's dream. There was massive interest in the initial robbery and much speculation at home and abroad on the whereabouts of the stone. Arthur had the story. He had the exclusive. In a subsequent interview, Arthur agreed that the international interest in the story enabled him to buy his first house. So, down time in the office. Desks were tidied, ashtrays emptied, newspapers read, crosswords attempted, sporting affiliations debated. For me, it was usually a queasy time, because, unlike my older colleagues, I hadn't yet developed the resilience required to survive the lunch-hour intake of three or four pints of beer and a couple of warmed pork pies.

Arthur quietly produced a paperback, the Kama Sutra by Vatsyayana, an ancient Hindu manual on human sexual behaviour. Its recent publication in paperback had caused a lot of debate in our part of the world, dealing as it did with all the delight and sensual pleasure to be sought and achieved in love-making, a unique and alien concept in our part of North East Scotland. It was rumoured to contain descriptions of 100 coital positions, which, a quick check confirmed, was ninety-eight more than anyone in the office had experienced.

Arthur's interesting choice of reading material was casually noted by us all, but kick-off at the football was in five minutes. We had all been issued with the games we had to cover. Arthur leant back in his chair, engrossed in this alien, erotic literature. Manuals on sex were available, if rare, but manuals on the *pleasures* of sex were unheard-of in east coast Scotland. Sex education in my case had been restricted to being handed a Church of Scotland leaflet complete with mysterious drawings of what looked like a source map of the River Nile, but were, in fact, drawings of male and female reproductive organs. My father's instruction was succinct: "Read that, digest it, and forget about it!" So, perhaps, there was room for a warmer, more relaxed approach. Concentrating fiercely, Arthur lifted his left leg up on to the front of his desk, pushing his canvas and steel tube chair into a dangerously acute angle. A page was turned. This was requiring some serious study. It's an interesting phenomenon, but one person's focus of attention can often act as a magnet to others. Some sensitive radar draws you to the one focal point. We were all pretending to be interested in something else. Some conversations continued uninterrupted, copy boys still buzzed around, but Arthur's involvement with his book was pulling focus across the office.

There was the slightest intake of breath as Arthur apprehensively raised his right leg up, placing it alongside its partner on the front of the desk, the chair tipping even further backwards. His concentration was now complete. As well as willingly submitting himself to the philosophy in the book, he was happily committing to it physically. His colleagues and underlings looked on, most surreptitiously, some blatantly.

Arthur sighed, leaned slightly back, and slowly, slowly, lifted his right leg up above his left leg. The tension was unbearable. We all realised he was going for this, completely devoted to whatever was on that page. He moved his raised right leg up and across and over the stationary left leg. No one breathed.

That's when the chair slid out from under him.

His feet and legs waved helplessly in the air for a moment and then bounced off the desk as the back of the chair smacked on to the floor. Surprisingly, he held on to the book, but whatever innovative techniques it had advocated, they would have to wait. A winded and disorientated Arthur scrambled untidily to his feet. He looked around the room at his astonished colleagues, then to the book in his hand. A comment, he felt, was called for.

"It cannae be done!" he declared, and threw the book across the room into the rubbish bin.

Then the football reports started arriving. Aberdeen versus Glasgow Celtic, Stenhousemuir versus Hamilton Academicals, normality was returning. Berwick Rangers against East Fife, Forfar Athletic versus Partick Thistle. Back to reality, everyone. This was more like it. This, we knew This, we could handle.

TUTTI FRUTTI

"The best television series made by BBC Scotland, ever."

That's my deeply biased opinion of the six-and-a-quarter hours of John Byrne's story of the Fabulous Majestics, Scotland's premier rock and roll band, and their less than earth-shattering silver jubilee tour.

I was wheeled in to meet Andy Park, the producer, and Tony Smith, the director, in 1986. The part? Bomba McAteer, drummer in the band. Like many other teenagers, I had been in a band while at school. I had bought a drum kit from the son of the owner of a cafe in my home town of Forfar, and set about learning to play. Sadly, I didn't have a teacher, so I had the fundamentals of kit-playing as wrong as it was possible to be.

Fast forward twenty years and after one meeting with Andy and Tony at the Acton Hilton, I get a recall for another meet. This is my version of *An Actor Prepares,* the Stanislavsky handbook for actors. I went out and bought a pair of drumsticks! Further extensive preparation led me to drummer Alan Grahame, with whom I'd worked on *Playschool,* for a single lesson. Alan it was who pointed out to me that my earliest, teenage theories on the art of drumming were completely, one hundred per cent, wrong. Wrong hands, wrong feet.

Just wrong. Nothing daunted, I sailed off to the second interview, drumsticks sticking optimistically from my back pocket. I was being unnecessarily flash. All the band members were going to be first-time musicians, I was told, each with his own personal tutor. Tony seemed more interested in whether my hair would grease flat into the required rocker style. I told him I had very talented hair that could do anything required of it. Andy said little but missed nothing.

Then it was a case of returning home and waiting.

I didn't have an agent to negotiate for me, so I was delighted to be told directly by Jonathan, the BBC booker or contracts negotiator, that I'd got the part. After the initial delight, I had to quickly calm down to talk about money. Years earlier, I had been so thrilled to be told that I had auditioned successfully to become a spear carrier with the Royal Shakespeare Company that they had to phone back the next day to say: "And by the way, you'll be paid eighteen pounds a week!" I was older and wiser now.

Jonathan, the booker, was patience personified. Over the next anxious ten days, he explained the contract, carefully leading me through the minefield of categories, fees and agreements. I would say "Not enough" and he'd go away and return with a rejigged offer. He must, eventually, have grown tired of "Not enough" when one day he said: "Stuart, is that your final word? Are you saying you cannot accept this offer, Stuart?"

"I'm sorry, Jonathan, but it's just not enough," I replied.

"Very well, then, Mr McGugan..."

Mr McGugan? Where had that come from? It had

been "Stuart" for the past two working weeks.

"I am now officially withdrawing our offer. Goodbye, Mr McGugan."

Click.

"Eh? What? Hello?"

I was mortified. I had just blown the job!

What to do? Who to call? I know. Tony Smith, the director. He's a fan...

I put a call in to the *Tutti Frutti* office in BBC Glasgow. There was a delay, and then it wasn't Tony who came on the line. It was Andy Park, the producer. Now, to call Andy Park "plain speaking" or "direct" is a wee bit of an understatement.

"Stuart, do you want this effing job or don't you?"

"Well, yes, of course, but..."

"But what?"

"There's not enough money."

"Not enough money? Not enough..? Listen, if you knew what the others are getting, you'd be rippin' ma effin' arm off!"

"But..."

"So do ye want it or don't ye?"

"Well, yes... Yes!"

"Right. That's that settled. Scripts on the way."

Click.

I wasn't even sure what I'd just agreed to, but I was IN!

....

I knew John Byrne as author of *The Slab Boys*, a semi-autobiographical play about work in the paint-mixing department of a linoleum factory. I knew it was powerful and poignant and very funny. But nothing prepared me for *Tutti Frutti.* Early the following Saturday morning, the postman delivered a bulky BBC package, containing episodes one to five. I took them back to bed with me. Towards noon I got out of bed. My chest and throat hurt. I had been laughing for three hours...

I come from the east coast of Scotland, in the country, and our humour reflects the surroundings. It's slow, and deadpan. Thanks to the huge historical Irish diaspora In Glasgow and the west coast, the humour there is fast, sharp and dark. The craic.

"Quick wi' the patter, that wan."

In the pubs, it's almost like a competition: who can be fastest with a cutting one-liner.

"Quick wi' the repartee."

John's scripts had all of that, and more. The show starts with a funeral, and over the next six-and-a-quarter hours there's a failed suicide, wife-bashing, a near-fatal car crash, serious stabbings with a bread knife, malicious wounding with a dentist's drill, a successful suicide, and to round off, a self-immolation on the stage of the Glasgow Pavilion. And it's funny!

I only really knew I had the part when the BBC delivered a handful of tapes of the show's music and a full drum kit to my house. Fortunately, relations with my neighbour were good.

I couldn't believe my brazen good fortune. Brilliant scripts, a drum kit all to myself, and rock and roll music. What's not to like?

Off to Glasgow.

Rehearsals began in a Boys' Brigade Hall at the foot of Byres Road, a street liberally and notoriously equipped with cafes, chip shops, off licences and pubs, and the natural spare-time habitat of artists and employees from the nearby BBC studios.

The original Majestics – Maurice Roëves, aka Vincent Diver, lead guitar; Jake D'Arcy, aka "Fud" O'Donnell, bass guitar; and myself were joined by Robbie Coltrane, aka Danny McGlone, on keyboards, along with our roadie Ron Donachie, aka Dennis Sproule, and we were introduced to our individual music coaches by our indefatigable musical director, George "Zoot" Money.

All the music for the show had been recorded by the start of rehearsals by professional musicians whose brief had been not to be too good. The Majestics were, after all, not a very good band.

There were more than a dozen tracks, and our job as actors was to be seen playing or hitting the right note at exactly the right time. This, I always thought, was much easier for the other guys than for me. The keyboard player's hands are rarely seen, and if a guitarist screws up, all he has to do is turn upstage, guitar and all.

There is no hiding place for the drummer. If the music calls for a cymbal and your drummer hits something else, the entire band's pre-recorded cover would be blown. To this end, the BBC found a tall, lugubrious Glaswegian drum maestro called Roy Sneddon to coach me. Always meticulous, Roy had heard and re-heard all the music, and then transposed it, painstakingly, on to paper. So total was my ignorance that it hadn't even occurred to me that drummers HAD written music. But there it was, laid out across five staves, bass on or under the bottom line, then up through snare and tom toms to the high hats and cymbals. So it wasn't a case of smacking away just as you felt like it. Now I had no excuse. I had all the parts written out for me. All I had to do was go away and practise.

As rehearsals proceeded, so the number of plasters on fingers grew. Maurice and Jake blistered up almost immediately, and my snare drum soon had bloodstains on it. But what a great life for an actor! Kidding on you were a rock and roll musician, rehearsing and bickering for hours with each other, aided and abetted by the irrepressible Zoot Money, encouraged by our director and our four tutors, and knowing, on top of it all, that six-and-a-quarter hours of fantastic dialogue were just waiting for us.

Rehearsals over, we were conveniently close to the renowned Ubiquitous Chip or the Cul de Sac pubs up the top end of Byres Road to continue getting into our rock and roll band characters. The actors prepare...

Roy Sneddon was a hard man to please. I had the kit, I had the tapes, I had Roy's music, I had the sticks, and I practised endlessly. I found all the drumming difficult, but *Great Balls Of Fire* was a killer. Our version of the Jerry Lee Lewis hit was even faster than his, and seemed to go on forever.

Late one Sunday evening, after hours of cramp-inducing hard labour, I felt, at last, that I'd cracked it. That simply meant I was hitting the right drum or cymbal on Roy's music at precisely the right time. There was, however, an instruction by Roy at the rousing end of the number that I didn't understand. "HEFT!" was written in capitals and in very heavy pencil. This was obviously drummer language, a secret from the uninitiated like me. I disturbed his evening by phoning him to tell him, excitedly, that I'd cracked *Great Balls Of Fire*. He was typically sanguine. "There's just one thing, though, Roy," I said. "Not being a drummer, I don't understand your instruction at the end. 'HEFT!' What does 'HEFT!' mean?"

"Stuart," he replied, "it means Hit Every Fucking Thing!"

....

Late for rehearsals one day, I was dashing down on to Byers Road when I nearly collided with one of the biggest guys I've ever seen. He seemed about seven feet tall, with a matching chest and thigh measurement. His hair was wild and long. Hiding behind a bushy beard, his face was dark and sunburned, his eyes deep set. I was reminded of nature programmes showing grizzly bears coming out of the forest in springtime and stretching on their rear legs to full height.

I stepped to the right. He stepped to his left. Stalemate. Go again. I stepped to my left. He stepped to his right. This two-step side-step quadrille could have gone on all day had my grizzly friend not stuck out both arms and grabbed me by my shoulders with hands the size of hams. To say my life flashed in front of me in that moment might be something of an exaggeration, but not much. His grip was painfully strong, he loomed above me and was well within range of delivering a swift and concussive Glasgow kiss to the top of my head. I could foresee pain and the imminent loss of both consciousness and plasma.

Instead, amazingly, he cocked his head to one side, smiled coyly and said: "Just once more, then I really must go!" I was poleaxed, not by the infliction of grievous bodily harm as I expected, but by the timing and delivery of this totally unexpected punch line.

Quick with the repartee. I was still hanging on to the railings, laughing, when I turned to see him lumbering uphill. Even from the back, you could tell by his heaving shoulders that he was pleased with himself.

I learned much later that "Just once more, then I really must go" is actually a quote from a Marx Brothers movie, which endears me even more to my hirsute two-step partner. The notion that he'd locked that one-liner away on the off-chance that some day, given the right circumstances, it might come in handy, is blissful. I am only too glad to have been his unwitting straight man. Go on yersel', son!

That's Glasgow for you.

The *Tutti Frutti* music rehearsals continued throughout the shoot. It was recognised that if we weren't utterly convincing as a band, then the six episodes, however beautifully crafted by Mr Byrne, would be seriously flawed. Our individual music coaches came with us. It must have been a slow and painful labour of love for Mr Sneddon to convert me into a believable drummer. I was desperately keen to do him and myself justice; I practised endlessly, but endeavour is no substitute for talent.

The closest Roy ever came to a compliment was at the recording of the Majestics' gig in Buckie town hall. The recording went on late into the night, with many takes from many angles. Roy came up to the kit. "I'm away tae my bed, Stuart. But see the second last time you done that?" I knew I'd been in good form for the previous takes, so I was anxious to hear Roy's opinion.

"Yes, Roy?"

He came closer to me and said quietly, "That was very nearly right!"

The plot line in Buckie was the discovery, during a Radio Buckie phone-in programme, of an illegitimate daughter of one of the band members, the result of a liaison during another tour twenty years earlier. The vengeful "Butcher Quine of Buckie" pursues her errant father – discovered to be Vinnie – and stabs him in the unmentionables. Early in the episode, it is thought that my character, Bomba, is the girl's father.

In a break in filming, I popped into the local Bank of Scotland to cash a cheque. The young man behind the counter accepted the cheque, recognised the name, and then looked up at me for what seemed a disconcerting length of time. With no change of expression, he intoned slowly and slightly threateningly: "Ma mother knows you......"

Turned out she'd been at Forfar Academy at the same time as me, but it was a worrying moment...

I last saw Roy a few months after *Tutti Frutti* went out, at a concert in the Edinburgh Festival given by the amazing Carol Kidd, a beautiful singer and interpreter of a song. Roy was on timpani. After the customary pleasantries, Roy said: "I don't know if you know this, Stuart, but Andy Park laid some of your playing over the master... and," he added, proudly, "none of the other boys done that!"

Now, I am well aware that Glasgow is the natural home of the wind-up and Roy's deadpan manner meant he could get away with it better than most, but my vanity refuses to allow me to believe that Roy was telling me anything but the absolute truth.

GUDDLING

Known to the genteel and uninitiated as "tickling", this is the long-lost skill of extracting a living fish from its natural habitat, a stream or river – or in this case, a burn – killing it, and taking it home and eating it. Guddling is what we did as kids. Tickling, in the main, means leaning over the bank of the chosen river with only the hands in the water.

Not us. We got on the "dookers" – sorry, swimming costumes – and shod with a pair of old plimsolls, went straight into the burn.

Trout are smart. And slippery. And fast. A trout will never swim under a stone or into a bank unless he has established his hiding place has an emergency exit. That's where being right in the burn helps the guddler. You can crouch over the stone, big and flat, with a hand over two exit holes. And if you suspect there's a fish in there, you can always block any extra exits with stones.

Then the battle of wits commences. Quietly, slowly, the guddler will attempt to turn the unsuspecting trout in the flowing current until the head nestles into his welcoming extended fingers. River weeds help disguise the forthcoming betrayal. Once enough of the head is grab-able, the finger trap shuts over the head and gills, and in one triumphant movement, guddler and fish dash for the bank, the second hand firmly grabbing the body of the wriggling prey. Once on dry land, the fish is dispatched by a swift jerk of the neck behind the head, and there he is, he's yours.

However often this happens, and as a kid I would spend whole days in the burn, this was the moment to look at your catch. Scottish burns produce beautiful brown trout. Only, it is not just brown. There's gold in there, crimson, blues and greens, flecks and flashes, a thing of extraordinary beauty. Sometimes this creature would twitch, or breathe its last before lying still on the grass, and it takes a moment to recover the callousness necessary to resume the hunt.

In *Lorna Doone*, by RD Blackmore, the hero, John Ridd, guddles for trout in the icy cold of Exmoor. To restore circulation to his frozen limbs, he thrashes himself with stinging nettles. It got cold in our burn at times, but never that cold.

There were few hazards to spoil an afternoon's guddling. The gamekeeper was one of them. And then there were eels. Always a menace, eels. They were usually to be found on bits of the burn where adjacent householders threw kitchen waste, so one's eel-alert antennae spiked. There is no more chilling sight – and it happened to a few of us – when about to insert the hand in pursuit of a trout under a stone, than to be greeted by the sleek, malevolent head of an eel, mouth open, teeth showing, slowly coming out towards your finger, waiting for it.

Gently, slowly, pretending you didn't want to feel under that stone anyway, the digit is retracted.

This is soundlessly accomplished, and then followed by a panicking run out of the burn up the bank, accompanied by a scream of swear words. Everything you touch, after that, under water, is going to feel like an eel. Sometimes you don't get your nerve back for a couple of days.

Another recognised hazard was the gamekeeper.

As guardian of the estate the burn ran through, grown-up poachers snaring rabbits and grown-up guddlers with nets were his usual target, but now and again, while busy trying to ease a trout out of a bank, you'd look up and into a broken double-barreled shotgun with the gamekeeper attached to the other end.

He never actually confiscated our catch, which he was rumoured to do with the bigger boys, but we had a ploy for that. As we worked our way upstream – always upstream to avoid muddying the bit of river you were working in – we would tie the trout we'd already caught with a bit of grass through the mouth and gills and fix them to somewhere safe on the river bank. You could tell – and show – the gamekeeper you hadn't caught anything. Then, obeying his admonishment, "Is it no' time ye went home for your tea..?", you could make your way home, picking up the caught and parked trout as you went.

That was a good day for a wee boy. A few fish to show a doting mother, and outsmarting the gamekeeper! Doesn't get much better. Even although, as you parted, the gamekeeper, worryingly, would say: "I ken you. And I ken yer faither…"

Letham, Angus, 1950-1966.

ENTER THE SUN KING

The opening of Trevor Nunn's production of *King Lear* at the Royal Shakespeare Company in Stratford-upon-Avon in 1968 was astonishing in its opulence and spectacle. RSC stalwarts David Waller and Sebastian Shaw opened the proceedings, playing Kent and Gloucester, and Norman Rodway was introduced as Gloucester's bastard son Edmund. So far, so brilliant.

Then Lear came on. The Sun King. Eric Porter, in flowing white beard and golden crown, was carried shoulder-high on to the stage sitting on an enormous black and gold-flecked throne by leather and fur-clad acolytes. The regal procession curved into centre stage accompanied by a resounding and thrilling brass fanfare composed by Guy Woolfenden. The lords and ladies of this land bowed low to their monarch. Power, wealth and authority pervaded the stage. Even we humble spear carriers were resplendent in our black and gold-flecked fur cloaks. The very spears were gold.

It was a Monday night performance. We'd all had the Sunday off.

The regal entourage stopped, centre stage. The spear carriers arced in a semi-circle around the throne as it was reverentially lowered, coming to rest at the same precise, carefully choreographed moment as the fanfare shrieked to a stop. The monarch glowered around his court. The last echoes of the fanfare sidled out of the theatre. Mr Porter waited for complete hush, both on stage and off, before uttering his first line, and into that profound, pin-drop silence an unidentified spear carrier's voice inquired of his neighbour:

"Have a nice weekend?"

It wasn't loud, but it carried. Some said as far as Row J in the stalls. The Sun King resignedly closed his eyes and sighed briefly. This was the last thing he needed at the start of four hours' hard thespian labour. He then slowly raised his crowned head, and glowered fiercely, first at the audience and then the actors, until everyone was silenced. Order restored, Mr Porter resonantly issued his first command of the evening.

"Attend the lords of France and Burgundy, Gloucester."

NOURISHING MARROWBONE JELLY

Commercial television arrived in the 1960s, and nothing was ever the same again.

In our village, the iron rule was: if you couldn't afford it, you did without. Then, hand in hand, the twin bad angels of commercial television and hire purchase sidled into the village. Buying on "the never never" became the norm. Put down a deposit and promise to pay a monthly sum for two, three, even four years, and the previously unattainable object of your desires, and the immediate envy of your neighbours, became yours.

The roads to my village were thick with delivery trucks loaded with fridges, washing machines, beds, blankets, pots, pans, cookers and TV sets. In front of the disapproving gaze of the older inhabitants of the village, accustomed only to frugality and solvency, luxury items sprouted in unfamiliar kitchens and living rooms like exotic fungi.

Feeding this frenzy were the advertisements and programmes of the new independent television companies. One advert, in particular, had unexpected consequences for the brother of a friend of mine. I would visit this family regularly, as I was in my teens, living away from home, in Aberdeen, for the first time. A colleague on the provincial newspaper where I worked kindly noticed this, and welcomed me into his home and family. So I'd watch television with him and his brothers of an evening, while their mother, a single mum, went to work in a local fish and chip shop.

It took me some time to notice that every so often during the evening's entertainment, my friend's teenage brother would, without warning, dash from the room, only to return, rather sheepishly, a few minutes later. I eventually plucked up the courage to ask why this happened. My friend looked blank for a moment and then said: "Aw, that? Sorry. It's been going on so long now we never notice it." He lowered his voice. "It's the 'nourishing marrowbone jelly'. He just can't stand it."

I had no idea what he was talking about, and said so.

"It's the advert. The advert on the telly. You know, the 'Pal Meat For Dogs' advert? Y'know, that's always bothered me. The ad says Pal dog food stands for 'Prolongs Active Life'. Well, of course it prolongs active life. It's food. If you didn't give it food, it would die. Nothing surer. It's like the Horlicks ad. It says Horlicks every evening before bed prevents 'night starvation'. What's that about? Have you ever heard of anyone suffering from, or dying from, 'night starvation'? Who makes this stuff up?

"Eh? Oh, the marrowbone jelly? Oh, that. That started weeks ago, when the advert first appeared," my friend continued. "At the end of the advert, when the man says 'Pal meat for dogs, with nourishing marrowbone jelly', there's this big close-up of a bone that's been cut in half, and then you see that out of it is slowly oozing this, well, big lump of jelly.

"That's when he first did it. My brother. As soon as

he saw that, he threw up on the carpet. Some strange connection. Auto-suggestion, I think it's called. The moment his eyes see the nourishing marrowbone jelly oozing out, he vomits! But now he's cute. As soon as the music for the ad starts, he's runs out the room."

I've wondered about this over the years. Surely, my friend's brother was not unique in his response to the big lump of jelly. Perhaps, all over the country, others learned, on hearing the introductory music to the advert, to dash from the room to save both their embarrassment, and the living room carpet.

Aberdeen, 1962.

THE DAY OF THE TRIFFIDS

My brothers Bill and Jim ran a flower shop in Montrose Road, Arbroath, for most of their adult lives.

It flourished, but I could see the hours were long and the work was hard, and you had to be nice to people all day; three good reasons for not joining them. To publicise the shop at Christmas, big brother Jim thought the good people of Arbroath would pay a lot of attention to a sandwich-board man – hitherto unseen in the town – so he had the boards built to his specification. Unfortunately, he ignored historical sandwich-board design of the small "Prepare to Meet thy Doom" variety, in favour of something much more impactful and robust.

Being a canny chap, he designed them with a dual purpose. When not being carried around town, they would double as billboards parked on the pavement outside the shop, and be strong and heavy enough not to be blown over. He then looked around for a sandwich-board man to carry the things. What he needed, he reckoned, was someone strong and fit, someone who would do anything for a small amount of money, and especially someone with a high embarrassment threshold. Guess who?

I couldn't get into them at first. They were made of

hardboard framed in wood and joined at the top by wide webbing shoulder straps, and ridiculously heavy. I discovered access could only be gained by squeezing between the boards, like entering a small, chunky tent. When I stood up, the boards reached to my shins and the backs of my calves.

So, just before Christmas, with the boards emblazoned with all the wonderful bargains to be had at the Flower Centre, big brother Jim patted me on the back and waved me off into town.

Arbroath is a famous fishing town on the east coast of Scotland, renowned for smoked haddock – smokies. Looking further east, the next land mass is Scandinavia. Beyond that, Russia, and at certain times of the year, that's where the wind comes from, straight across the North Sea, hard, sharp and bitter.

That's when my troubles began. At the start of my maiden voyage, I had already discovered that normal steps were just not possible. The front board clipped my shins, and then the back board caught me a nasty smack in the calf. I tottered downhill, the boards beating a relentless tattoo fore and aft. To escape, I turned sharp left, only to catch the freezing, jagged wind from the Russian steppes in my back. Now resembling a yacht in full sail, I unwillingly picked up speed, and soon had sturdy Arbroathians throw themselves into the road to avoid painful collisions. The good news about the bargains available from my brothers' shop was ignored as pedestrians were forced to decide between being run over in the street or concussed on the pavement.

Angry expletives filled the air. The gusty Siberian wind and icy pavements propelled me drunkenly towards the High Street and the traffic. I could swear the boards were drawing blood. Narrowly avoiding an ashen-faced mother and her pram, I pirouetted into a newsstand, which in turn spun me across the pavement, smack into a lamppost. I grabbed it and hung on for dear life, only a board's length from the cars and trucks in the busy High Street.

Ignoring the awful language from the now-fully recovered mother with the pram, I slowly unwrapped myself from the lamppost, and took stock. My modish Robin Hood-style hat, all the rage at the time, was gone. My shins were singing with pain while my calves throbbed in sympathy. The webbing had chafed my neck and my knuckles were skinned, probably from the newsstand. I was looking and feeling awful. Bashed and bleeding, the morning had been a disaster. Surely things couldn't get any worse. No?

At precisely this point, the entire population of Arbroath High School, all classes, pupils aged between eleven and seventeen, hundreds of them, complete with teachers, turned the corner in front of me on their way to their annual Christmas church service. None of them was looking forward to an hour in a cold church, so any diversion was welcome. Children can be very cruel.

The comments were not subtle, and there were many of them, displaying a level of inventiveness and coarseness I would not have thought possible from such young minds. I swear even the staff joined in. My high embarrassment threshold was thoroughly breached. I retrieved my Robin Hood-style hat from the gutter on the way back to the shop. It was, like me, bedraggled and much abused. Big brother Jim accepted my resignation with good grace, before confessing he was surprised I had made it as far as the High Street. The boards served the shop well for many years, parked outside on the pavement. As far as I know, they were never carried again.

....

John Wyndham published *The Day of the Triffids,* a post-apocalyptic science fiction novel in 1951. A meteor shower blinds most people in the world, and then an aggressive plant starts killing the survivors. The novel was filmed in 1962 with Howard Keel and Nicole Maurey, and it came to Arbroath a year later. My brothers were too busy to read novels or go to the cinema at that time. All their energies went into establishing The Arbroath Flower Centre as a viable and successful business.

Jim was serving late on Saturday afternoon when a customer, obviously slightly the worse for wear, navigated the shop entrance and made his uncertain way to the counter. Beckoning Jim to come closer, he breathed conspiratorially and alcoholically: "Heh, pal, do ye huv any o' them triffid plants?"

"Eh?"

"Triffid plants," repeated the customer, a little more loudly, as if the increased volume would make it easier for Jim to understand. "Ye know... Ah've just seen them."

"Triffid, you say? I don't think so," said Jim, who prided himself on his knowledge of things horticultural. "Triffid? What do they look like?"

"Ah," said the customer, believing now that he was getting somewhere, "They're about twice the size o' me. And they blind ye!"

"Come again?"

"Ay, they have these pods and when they hit ye wi

one o' them, ye go blind and they kill ye." He tried to demonstrate with his arm but gave up when his balance was affected. The customer tried to re-focus on the shopkeeper's face. There was a pause.

"It's fur the wife," he added gravely.

Jim eventually had to confess. "No... sorry. I don't think so. I don't think we have one of them."

The customer looked disappointed.

"However," said Jim, always the salesman, "I can let you have a Venus fly catcher."

The customer brightened up. "What does that do?" he asked.

"It... It, em, catches flies."

"Catches flies?"

"Yes."

Another pause, then: "Naw... naw. That's no use tae me. That's no' what Ah'm lookin' for at all."

The customer turned ponderously, then let his upper body weight propel him towards the door.

"Flies, is it," he muttered on the way out. "Catches bloody flies..."

Arbroath, 1966.

IRISH SPRING

So there was I, a Scotsman, playing an Irishman, filming in New Zealand, making an advert for soap. German soap.

Irish Spring was a fashionably "marbled" anti-bacterial toilet soap manufactured by Colgate Palmolive that sold remarkably well in Europe, especially Germany. The big selling point of Irischer Fruhling was that it kept you fresh – ie. smelling of soap, not of yourself – for many hours. I had already made one advert for them in County Kerry, southern Ireland. This depicted a day in the life of the advertising world's typical Irish lad. Up at the crack of dawn with his girlfriend to ride his pony and trap halfway across the island to attend a ceilidh well into the wee small hours of the following day. The dance at the ceilidh involved a lot of holding one's arms aloft, which your typical Irish lad could do without fear of social ostracisation as he'd bathed in the fragrant, long-lasting Irish Spring before setting off.

The location was stunningly beautiful, especially in late summer. The hedgerows consisted of fuchsia and honeysuckle, which looked and smelled wonderful. That combination, in the soft evening with the added distant smell of someone's fire burning peat, was almost hallucinogenic. My companion on this early-morning call was a nervous German girl with cascades of ginger wavy hair – advertising's typical Irish colleen – and, sadly, a drink problem. We were helped on to the pony and trap and awaited loudspeakered instructions from the director and camera crew, halfway up the adjacent hill.

"Ready? And action!" Clip clop, off we went.

Now, I don't know what your average trap pony's diet is. I do know, however, that whatever our pony had been given for breakfast, it was producing an extraordinary amount of equine flatulence. It wasn't so much clip clop, more clip fart clop fart clip fart clop. My German colleague was not happy with either the noise or the smell, or indeed being very far from the nearest drink. Perched in a pony and trap, you are very, very close to the business end of a pony's digestive system. She demanded we stop. A harassed assistant who had been hiding out of shot in a ditch was instructed to calm things down and return us to first position for a retake.

A three-point turn is a tricky manoeuvre at the best of times, but in a pony and trap, on a very narrow Irish country lane with a ditch on either side, and with a farting horse and an increasingly hysterical German actress, we were soon way behind schedule. After every subsequent take, and there were many of them, my colleague would ask: "We go now for a little drink?" Only later did I realise that our director must have known of this young lady's problem. He'd made very sure the important, romantic travelling shot was completed miles away from the nearest pub. Once back at the ceilidh, though, the drink was flowing freely.

Assembled in the base hotel were a couple of

coachloads of the most extraordinary-looking extras. I could see the caster's brief had been to supply lots of advertising's typical "characterful" Irish faces.

What we had was the entire clientele from Dublin RentAnUgly. Like the old music hall joke, there were scars and broken noses and cauliflower ears everywhere – and that was just the women.

Also, they'd been in the hotel for hours. The travelling shot had taken much longer than anticipated, and it was a ceilidh after all, so what else was there to do but drink? By the time we joined them, the non-speaking artistes had gone through the known stages of inebriation: Happiness, Extreme Happiness, Maudlin Sentimentality, Resentment and Violence.

A false waterfall had been set up in the hotel grounds, around which the ceilidh was to take place, and through which some of the romantic, dancing, arms-in-the-air shots, plus the all-important Irischer Fruhling pack shot of the green marbled soap out of its box were planned. How he managed it I'll never know, but our director filmed the dancing and avoided the fighting.

He got his pack shot and missed the waterfall leaking all over the place, and he caught me and my now completely wrecked German colleague gazing happily and romantically at each other. In love and still smelling of an Irish Spring.

....

Months later, the agency called again. The clients, Colgate Palmolive, were happy with the County Kerry ceilidh and wanted to make another 30-second ad as soon as possible. Trouble was, now we're in the middle of winter. "No problem," came the reply. "Where in the world looks like County Kerry in the summertime in the middle of a European winter?" So, on the day after Boxing Day, I found myself on a plane bound for New Zealand. Two changes of plane and several continents later, I was booked into the Intercontinental Hotel, Auckland, while the director and cameraman hired a helicopter and set off to view the proposed locations.

New Year's Eve was celebrated in the hotel's rooftop restaurant. For pudding, I ordered the "sorbet surprise", which was delivered to the table in a sort of two-tier, one soup plate atop another soup plate arrangement. "What's the surprise?" I asked the harassed waitress. "This is," she replied, and splashed water on to some dry ice crystals surrounding the sorbet glass. The whole thing immediately gushed dry ice out on to the table and on to the floor. I was horrified. It would only take one inebriated Kiwi – and remember, this was New Year's Eve – to mistake the dry ice for genuine smoke and we could have a full-scale panic on our hands. We were on the top floor. This could be an antipodean "Towering Inferno". Luckily, these Hogmanay New Zealanders were concentrating on enjoying themselves far too much to panic about a little bit of smoke.

It's a brilliant country, New Zealand, and the timing of my visit could not have been better. Late in the previous year, I had started jogging, to try to work off weight gained when I'd stopped smoking. To suddenly and unexpectedly find myself out running in blazing sunshine in January seemed like a reward for my good intentions, and in a country where, it seemed to me, any spare time was spent either up in the hills or on the beach, instead of in front of a television set. Our main location was near Cambridge in North Island, and perversely and illogically, the shoot was to take place on a huge, bare, hillside-sized rock, which, this being advertising, would now be covered in turf. I was learning not to ask questions while doing commercials. Any logical person would find a normal hill with grass already growing on it to shoot on, but not Colgate Palmolive, and not our director.

Wagonloads of turf arrived and were laid all over the bare rock. An old-fashioned cast-iron water pump was found in a local museum, borrowed and made practical. This was placed on top of the turfed rock. Very Jack and Jill.

In the gaps between the turfs, hundreds of white and yellow flowers were planted: colours long associated subliminally with freshness. At the end of the day, and with everyone, even the representatives of the clients helping out, we were good to go. Then for the next forty-eight hours, the essential sun, the main reason for us all being there, disappeared. And by the time it reappeared, all the flowers, unwatered and planted on a rock, had died.

More flowers were ordered and planted. Lesson learned, the grass, flowers and rock were regularly watered. We could start shooting.

My co-star, if that's not too grand a title for a youngster in a TV commercial, was Chloe Salaman from London, dark-haired, pretty, and very sexy. She sits next to the well in a beautifully cut blouse and skirt, idly dipping her fingers in the water.

Enter me, halfway up the floral, turfed rock. I'm dressed head to toe in very hot, hairy and itchy tweed, the German wardrobe master's idea of Irishness. For reasons never fully explained, I'm also trying to walk up the rock in a pair of wooden clogs.

"ICH HABE ETWAS NEUES FUR DICH!" I exclaim.

"I have something new for you!"

She says nothing.

"ES DUFTET HERTZHAFT FRICHT," I continue.

"It smells wonderfully fresh!"

"WIE EINE ERISHERFRUHLING?"

"Like an Irish Spring?" she asks, out of nowhere.

"JA!" I reply, producing a cake of the stuff from behind my back.

And that's it. Four weeks there and back, countless pounds to make, and that, plus a stills photograph session for magazines, is it.

The all-important pack shot was a classic. I was asked to take a very sharp knife and cut a curl off the marbled green and white soap to enable our cameraman initially to shoot the soap, then zoom through the curl into the beauty of Lake Karapiro in the background.

Given my time on *Play School,* where we were regularly asked to coolly make and build things in close-up, the pack shot was done very quickly and efficiently. However, Colgate Palmolive were not satisfied. Weeks after we'd all returned home, I had a call saying the clients in Germany were not happy, and the pack shot would have to be done again. The soap, apparently, was "not marbled enough".

Thoughts of a return to New Zealand were quickly quashed. Specially marbled soap was being manufactured and flown into a studio in Soho, London, and could we do the new pack shot there, please? Sure enough, a huge picture of Lake Karapiro was to be used instead of the real thing, and there in the studio were a dozen or so heavily marbled cakes of soap, specially made and shipped by the clients.

Unfortunately, the assistant floor manager had been given the task of making the soap look virginally shiny, and had coated them all lightly in sunflower oil. Come the take, with my sharp knife at the ready to cut the magic curl, a firm grip on the treated soap made it squirt out of my grasp like a live trout and on to the floor. As usual with unforeseen problems in a studio, we all went back to the pub and left stage management to sort it out. On our return, the soap wasn't as shiny, but at least I could hold on to it,

Sadly, marbled soap and Irischer Fruhling lost its popularity. The soap-buying public moved on, and I suspect the account managers at Colgate Palmolive advertising were only too pleased.

New Zealand 1976.

AT THE PAPERIE

After my sudden departure from Bruce's Commercial College in Dundee, due to the unpleasantness in the typing class, I had to look for gainful employment. The local paper, the *Kirriemuir Herald,* was looking for a reporter. I got the job.

Kirriemuir is set in the foothills of the glens of the county of Angus, north of Edinburgh, south of Aberdeen, and fifteen miles inland from Dundee on the east coast of Scotland. Agriculture and jute mills were the main employers. JM Barrie, author of *Peter Pan,* was born there.

Although Kirrie only had about five thousand inhabitants, it boasted two weekly newspapers, the *Herald* and the *Free Press,* sustained not by commercial viability, but by deep and historic rivalry. It was always a challenge filling the eight broadsheet pages of "The Paperie," or, as it was more caustically known, "The Two Minutes' Silence", with the publishable goings-on in the town.

My boss was Willie Ogilvy. He was essentially the foreman printer, with posters, invitations, raffle tickets being the main business income. Willie had spent so many years feeding paper into inky printers that he had a finger-licking tic that persisted even when he wasn't at work. You soon got used to it. He also knew everyone. Bruce Purchase was our sole Linotype operator, and Ally Bruce, a contemporary of mine from the old Forfar Academy days, was the apprentice printer.

The Paperie's building would be condemned nowadays as unfit for human occupation. Brick walls, reeking stove, leaking corrugated iron roof, open shelves piled high with reams of different kinds and colours of paper, oil cans, oily rags, mugs, bits of food, full ashtrays, and not a fire extinguisher to be seen. Either Willie or I could occupy the paper's offices. We couldn't both sit down in there at the same time.

I was interviewed for the job standing up in the office. Willie checked the few credentials I possessed, seemed happy with them, and phoned up another local paper to find out what my pay should be. "So yer saying for a beginner it's three ten?" said Willie into the phone. Then to me: "That OK with you?"

"Yes, fine," I replied, trying to do the quick mental arithmetic. Wow! My first job in 1962 and three hundred and ten pounds a year? That's six quid a week! A lot of money then for a sixteen-year-old recently chucked out of his school and then Bruce's Commercial College with not a qualification in sight. So you can imagine my disappointment when my first week's pay packet contained not the anticipated six pounds, but three pound notes and ten shillings... Three ten a week.

Still, I had a job.

Kirriemuir, which also encompassed Northmuir, Southmuir, Westmuir, but strangely no Eastmuir, is built on a series of very steep hills, all of which had to be negotiated in pursuit of a story. Countless times I'd be told, after schlepping all the way up to an address in

Northmuir, "Na, na laddie, it's no' me ye want. It's Mrs McBogle doon in Southmuir... I swear they used to tell each other I was on my way, not necessarily by telephone – they didn't all have a telephone – but by that strange small town bush telegraph that was the blight of this young reporter's ambition, as well as costing a fortune in shoe leather.

There were lighter moments. A local firm's annual staff party in the town hall had decided on an Elizabethan theme, with all the serving wenches dressed in big flouncy dresses over lots of underskirts. Wench after wench proudly told me how many underskirts the boss had asked them to wear to bulk up the top garment. "And how many underskirts do you have on?" I asked one of the older ladies. "Nane at a', laddie, " she replied, "I jist back-combed ma hair!"

Exit red-faced wonder-boy reporter.

An ante-room in the town hall served as a courthouse for minor misdemeanours when they occurred, and the local police were always happy to welcome the press. One Monday, I was given the nod for a hearing involving one of the more reckless local drunks, who had been found urinating in the alleyway between the Airlie Arms and the Ogilvy Arms hotels – a happy hunting ground for the constabulary.

"Drunk and disorderly" was the charge, but yer man – we'll call him Tam – was disputing the charge with the baillie, or magistrate, on an unusual technicality. "I ken my rights. Ye cannae have a court on the Sabbath," he claimed, when asked how he pleaded.

"Eh?" said the baillie.

"This is Sunday," insisted Tam. "Ye cannae have a court on the Sabbath."

"But Tam," said the sergeant, trying to be helpful, "this isnae Sunday. It's Monday!"

"Awa'," said Tam. "Look. When wis I lifted?"

The sergeant consulted his book. "The accused was apprehended while urinating in the close atween the Ogilvy Arms and the Airlie Arms hotels on Saturday night at 10.50 pm. He was arrested and taken into custody, with some difficulty, at 11.30 pm."

"See?" said Tam. "Saturday night. And noo it's Sunday."

"Tam," said the sergeant. "Ye slept a' the wey through Sunday. Ye woke an' roared a few times, but maistly ye just slept!"

"Ye're haverin'," said Tam.

"Ah'm no' haverin'," replied the sergeant. "Ye banged at the door at..." He checked his book. "...Half past six this morning, shoutin' fur yer breakfast."

"Sunday mornin'," insisted Tam.

"Naw, Tam, Ah'm tellin' ye," said the sergeant, "it's Mond…"

"Stop. Stop. Wait a minute," said the baillie. He reached under his pile of official papers and produced a copy of the *Dundee Courier and Advertiser*. "Show him this."

The sergeant handed the paper to Tam, who stared at the top of the front page for a long time, taking it in. If it's in the *Courier*, then it must be true.

"Well, fuck me," he said at last. Then, again: "Dammit!"

"Ah'll no' have that language in my court," said the baillie. "Weel Tam, how dae ye plead?"

Tam looked straight at the baillie and the bench.

"Guilty, yer honour."

"Fined ten shillings," said the baillie. "Two weeks tae pey. And Tam..."

"Whit?"

"Next time ye go oot on the bevvy, tak' a diary wi' ye!"

Kirriemuir 1961.

OH, MR PORTER!

For a young actor in 1968, the Royal Shakespeare Company in Stratford-upon-Avon was an exciting place to be. Trevor Nunn was in his first season completely in charge at the tender age of 28, succeeding Peter Hall, who was off to help create the National Theatre in London. And much to my surprise, I was in the company. My second job, and nine months after leaving drama college in Glasgow. Only a humble spear carrier, to be sure, but I was in the Royal Shakespeare Company.

And me from Letham!

Our first production was to be *King Lear*, with Eric Porter as the king, and Trevor Nunn directing. Mr Porter was on something of a roll, having just received national acclaim for playing the bullying misogynistic Soames Forsyte in a 26-part BBC television adaptation of John Galsworthy's *Forsyte Saga*. It was such a popular series that on Sunday evenings the times of some church services had to be changed to avoid clashing with Mr Porter.

There were many theatrical heavyweights in the cast of *King Lear* besides Eric Porter, but regardless of status, we were all issued with identical track suits for rehearsals and company games. These games were the forerunners of today's "bonding" exercises in big business. In order to function as a cohesive unit, instead of a ramshackle collection of differing talents, and to develop trust, confidence and reliance, strange techniques were employed to "bind" us. One involved chucking a big fluffy ball across a circle and shouting out the first name of the chucker and receiver. Others were more intimate and bizarre.

These sessions always seemed to be led by enthusiastic, strident American girls, urging us on. Any tendency to take the games less than seriously was frowned upon, mainly because in all of these exercises there is a crucial giggle point that has to be negotiated, and suppressed.

In the large, bare rehearsal room, all twenty-odd similarly-clad members of the cast, enthusiastic youngsters through to cynical veterans, were divided into small groups with instructions to stand in a circle, looking inwards. Strict silence was observed.

Slowly, slowly, shoulder to shoulder, looking down, we were asked to become aware of the rhythms, movement and breathing of our neighbours. Spookily, each group picked up a sound, a sway, an in-breath, an exhalation.

With mounting tension, the small, personal sounds combined within the groups and slowly began to build. Something was happening, although none of us knew quite what.

Mr Porter, our leading man, was a renowned and expert timer of a line.

Shoulder to shoulder, eyes cast downwards, the cast approached the giggle point of no return. That's when Mr Porter spoke. In a loud, mock-Yorkshire voice he announced: "WHEN I WERE A LAD, WE CALLED THIS 'SHOW US YER COCK'!"

The place erupted. Twenty-odd track-suited thespians exploded hysterically out of their circles. Some collapsed on to the floor, others fell into each other's arms, all were helpless with laughter. Mr Porter looked on in amazement at the chaos his innocent one-liner had caused.

Mr Nunn thought briefly about firing Mr Porter, then dismissed the idea. He was King Lear, after all.

No more games were risked for more than a week. But even then, as now, when the inevitable giggle point of any team-building exercise approaches, I can still hear Mr Porter declaim "When I were a lad..." and hysterics have to be painfully suppressed.

Stratford-upon-Avon,1968.

ALLAN CAMPBELL AND ME

Allan Campbell was my best pal in Letham. Allan was the village policeman's son, the third of four: Ian, Bill, Allan and Jimmy. He was brave, kind and mischievous. We had some amazing – and dangerous – times together. And him being the policeman's son could come in handy sometimes.

Early in the long summer holidays from school, Allan travelled the twelve miles or so to my home in Westmuir from Letham. My family had moved to a bigger house. We decided – again – to play Jerries versus British and re-enact the Second World War. First, though, supplies would have to be purloined. When my mother wasn't looking, I sneaked into the pantry and stole a big tin of peaches and a can opener. Then we had to arm ourselves. Allan was happy with a broom handle for a rifle, but I had found something quite special: an entire table leg with two jagged slices of the original table still joined to it at right angles, perfect for a machine gun.

Before letting battle commence, however, we prised open the lid of the peaches tin and scoffed the lot, safe in the woodshed at the top of the garden. Before Allan took off to hide and be the Jerry, I noticed a length of string had somehow fixed itself on to the bottom of my tommy gun, quite spoiling the effect. No problem. I put the gun on the ground, string side up, and picked up the hand axe used for chopping kindling wood. I teed up the string and swung at it with the axe.

The next bit happened, I swear, in slow motion. As the axe was descending, a gust of wind blew the string off my tommy gun. I looked on, fascinated, as the index finger of my left hand moved to push the string back into position, while the axe continued its descent. The axe caught the string as planned, then, unplanned, the end of my finger. I yelled in pain, grabbed the bleeding digit in my right hand and took off towards the house and my mother.

Now, all mothers of all wee boys are accustomed to the occasional drama, where it is necessary to calm the child and then persuade him to let you see where the hurt is, gently easing the protecting hands away from the painful bit. What my mother was not prepared for, I found out later, was a spray of blood squirting up from the end of my nearly-severed digit. There was, as they used to say in The Sweeney, "claret everywhere".

With Allan ducking and weaving behind me, trying not to miss anything, my mother, joined by my big brother Jim, eventually managed to stem the bleeding and put a temporary dressing on the cut. Then shock set in.

"I'm going to be sick!"

My mother shoved a basin under me, and then looked on in perplexity as her son, so recently injured in a frightening domestic accident, now appeared to be vomiting a seemingly endless supply of tinned peaches.

Allan, bless him, could offer no explanation for this when cross-examined. Arrangements were made for

Jim to drive me to the nearest hospital in Forfar in his recently-acquired Ford Anglia. So, with my hand bandaged and wrapped in a towel, we set off.

"Don't you go getting blood on the seats," Jim warned.

Allan was dropped back home, and then we had to wait for ages in the local A and E. I was given an assortment of injections before the doctor unbandaged the finger. He was tutting to himself and flapping the tip of the finger up and down.

"Is it bad, doctor? Are ye going to have to cut it off?" I asked, genuinely interested.

"What? Eh? No, no, son. You'll need something to pick your nose with!"

So I still have the finger, with a neat scar almost all the way round the top of it, and although Allan and I never got to finish our game of Jerries and British, I think I'm entitled to call it a war wound.

Westmuir, 1968.

CHAFF AND BRAN

I wonder if William Shakespeare, who was an actor before he hit the big time, was ever a spear carrier? I suspect he had never experienced being an extra or a two-line walk-on, because he describes the status and craft of spear carrying so scathingly in *Troilus and Cressida,* which was part of the 1964 season in Stratford-upon-Avon.

Cressida first sets eyes on Troilus when he returns, with all the other Trojan heroes and their minders, from another hard day fighting the Greeks on the Dardan Plain. As the Trojan nobility and their guards file past, Cressida asks her guide Pandarus who they are and what rank they hold. Pandarus is eloquent and gushing in his praise of the heroes, all actors with recognisable parts and mentioned as such in the glossy programme, but he's scathing when he gets to us, the spear carriers.

"Crows and daws," he proclaims. "Porridge after meat. Chaff and bran!" he sneers.

The purveyor of the well-crafted insult, our author. It's bad enough being a walk-on schlepping back to Troy and the barracks and the wife and family covered in mud and blood after another day's graft on the Dardan Plain, but to be told you are "porridge after meat", and "chaff and bran", well, it just takes the heart from you. Good mind to go sick tomorrow...

We spear carriers were so incensed by our casual dismissal in *Troilus* that when we came together to present one-act plays in our lunch hour, we named ourselves "The Chaff and Bran Repertory Company", and when we formed a football team, we were the Chaff and Bran XI.

In *Troilus,* we spear carriers were kept busy in the early qualifying round battles, but were much busier later in the play, when the two armies, Greek and Trojan, clash in the decider. Our director had decided that each of the Trojan heroes should individually fight the opposing Greek heroes, and to this end, each hero, accompanied by one back-up lieutenant, had rehearsed and choreographed separate sword and shield fights.

The background to this was smoke and dust and drums and trumpets. The spear carriers, in the interests of economy, played both armies. It was a marvellous spectacle. The Dardan Plain was heaving with noise and action. Unfortunately, one matinee, things went slightly awry.

Troilus was off. In theatrical parlance, that means he had missed his cue to go on stage. Actually, he had momentarily lost the place, convinced that he wasn't on again for ages. That would explain why he was found chatting in the backstage scene dock with half a pint of Guinness in his hand. And he was Trojan hero number one, scheduled to fight Greek hero number one in the opening bout.

Back on stage, Greek hero number one and his minder leapt fiercely from the wings, roaring and ready to do bloody battle with Troilus, Trojan hero number one, so it was a bit of an anti-climax when they found they were on their own. On the other side of the stage, Trojan hero number two spotted the hiatus, and in the mistaken belief that the show must go on, decided to replace his absent boss, and leapt equally fiercely into battle, unfortunately forgetting that they had rehearsed two entirely different fights.

Meanwhile, the smoke and the drums and the alarums of battle kicked in, vainly trying to camouflage the fact that the two combatants and their acolytes weren't actually hitting each other very much. Even with the smokescreen, the four warriors were giving a very good impression of a slow-motion Tai Chi exhibition, and when they eventually gave it up as a bad job and left, that forced Trojan hero number three and Greek hero number two onstage to repeat the embarrassment.

Backstage was pandemonium. Mud and blood were being sloshed around everywhere as the spear carriers tried to decide whether they were on the winning or losing army, or maybe both, and which side to run on from. Anxious kettle drummers tried to shield their skins from flailing spears and swords. Trumpeters protected their lips and teeth from the chaos by pointing at each other.

The mayhem continued until everyone had tried at least once to fight someone else. Sometimes even twice. Eventually, when we had run out of heroes and acolytes and also options, the play lurched back on track.

I had friends in, watching that afternoon, and later, in the Dirty Duck, I apologised for the chaotic battle scenes. They didn't know what I was talking about. What they had seen was a lot of smoke and noise, spear carriers madly running about, as well as endless duels of confused, stylised sword waving, and they had loved it.

Stratford-upon-Avon, 1968.

MY WEE SISTER

"Yes, of course. I'll see to it straightaway. They'll be ready for you whenever you want to pick them up." My wee sister Margaret was on the phone, sounding very serious, but she was smiling. The smile disappeared.

"Gary!"

She knew this moment would come. She had known from the moment her second son had presented her, proud as Punch, with a fine pair of fresh, recently caught rainbow trout. Gary had always been a hunter. Nothing was safe from him, and here he was, not even in his teens, bringing home the spoils. But his mother Margaret, born and bred in the country, knew that rainbow trout were not native to the rivers and burns in Angus, in east Scotland. Brown trout lived in Angus waters. And she knew that, sooner or later, she'd hear more about this.

The irate caller, a newcomer to the village, had been told that Gary – whose shock of red hair was a giveaway – had been spotted guddling in her expensively-installed ornamental pond and stream, and on checking up, she'd discovered her rainbow trout population diminished by two. Margaret had anticipated this, had gutted and cleaned the fish, and popped them in the freezer, ready for pickup. The irate caller, unabashed, did eventually collect the two frozen trout. Margaret was mother to five boys and at the same time ran a flower shop in nearby Forfar. She was dyslexic, a condition undiscovered by the education authorities in Angus when she was of school age. Like many fellow-sufferers, she was labelled "stupid". This only made her more determined to prove them wrong, and also made her fiercely protective of her children, some of whom had inherited the condition.

She had her own way of dealing with the trickier aspects of running a business, a foreign land to the casual visitor. On a whiteboard at the rear of the shop she'd write the names of the plants she needed to order from her Dutch supplier. I can only invite you to suggest what a dyslexic would make of the plant names *Tradescantia Zebrina* or *chamaemelum nobile*. The whiteboard looked like a bad hand at Scrabble, but Margaret understood it, and made it work.

When she retired recently, the five boys were concerned. What would she do now?

How would she spend her time and her amazing energy?

Answer? A springer spaniel pup called Murphy.

Job done.

BENIDORM!

It's a raffle, your chances of getting an acting job or not getting an acting job. Actors are always fond of saying "Then I was offered the role of...", when what they mean is "I joined another dozen or so actors, most of whom I knew because of our similar backgrounds, history and experience, to audition for this one part". While waiting your turn to read from the script, at this time usually in front of the director, casting director and sometimes the writer, it's an opportunity to catch up with the usual suspects – old mates, competitors and sworn enemies – and bullshit about how well everything's been going since the last time we all met.

The audition or reading experience is fraught with hazards, and one off-the-cuff remark can either get you the job or scupper your chances entirely. For example, do not, however ghastly the script is, return it to the director with the innocent and sincere query: "And when are you expecting the next draft?" That is audition suicide.

These days, most auditions are with only one person and a video camera, making sure that all your unintentional gaffes then get played to the widest possible audience back at the production office. And, even more recently, you are asked to audition either online or, worse still, to your own telephone. The audition for the part of Wink McAndrew in *Benidorm* was held in London in front of the casting director and a camera, as the writer and director were already in Spain halfway through the series.

Wink had an early Glasgow-accented line to an uncomprehending Spanish hotel receptionist, who said innocently: "This is just a noise to me. Are you speaking English?"

"Of course Ah'm speakin' English," replied Wink, to which I added the Glasgow soubriquet of "Ya numpty!". Derren Litten, the show's writer, was notorious for not permitting any additions or alterations to his work, but I'm told "Ya numpty!" got me the part.

Benidorm itself was an eye-opener. I had never met the Great British holidaymaker let loose abroad, and in Benidorm there was something for everyone, with added alcohol. Bars for drinkers from everywhere, Irish bars, north and south, Welsh bars, English bars, Scots bars, and for the more particular, Scouse bars, Geordie bars, Glasgow bars; every country, every city – booze for all and at rock bottom prices. Cirrhosis by the sea. Although I was billeted on the eighth floor of one of the posher, quieter hotels, even up there the night air was filled with raucous, no-holds-barred karaoke from many different sources, ending only at chucking-out time with hysterical screams and shouts as the punters made their wobbly way to bed.

Next day at work, I mentioned to my make-up lady that I'd noticed what great care the resort took to accommodate holidaymakers with walking difficulties, given the amazing number of mobility scooters in the town. She snorted derisively while carefully sculpting the elaborate comb-over I'd requested for Wink. "They can walk," she said. "They just can't be arsed!"

"Surely not," I said. "There's just too many of them."

"They can walk, don't you worry," she replied. "They book the holiday, one week, two, then they book the scooter. Saves them the effort."

A couple of days later, with time off, I made my way to the seashore around 12.30, time for the all-inclusive lunches to be served in all the hotels up from the beach. Heading up the hill, two, three, four abreast they came. A mobility scooter Derby. It was like the start of the old Le Mans 24-hour endurance race. Tight-lipped, grim-faced overweight James Hunts, pursued by equally determined tubby Stirling Mosses, all chasing pole position for the lunch counter.They parked up, then legged it into the restaurants, not running exactly, but rolling effortlessly, swinging the weight from side to side until maximum velocity was reached through the dining room doors and on to the appetiser and starter tables. Game on!

I conceded all this on my next working day to my make-up lady. "Told you!" was her reply.

All the pool-side activity in the series was filmed in a cordoned-off section of a working hotel pool, with holidaymakers just around the corner. To get to the location, the cast and crew had to make their way through what became known as "lard alley", or the sun lounger section. In rows, blindingly white holidaymakers were slowly cooking and browning, basted with oil and lotions against the sun.

This resembled a shiny, pink, human version of a David Attenborough documentary on sea lions or walruses. Stretching and scratching, they left their loungers only to slide into the pool, or to order more drinks. Here, too, lunchtime was observed with dedicated reverence. Ten minutes or so before the off, peckishness set in, and the colony began to bestir itself.

One particularly bulky lounger found the physics involved in getting out of the sunbed trickier than anticipated. Eventually, after several unsuccessful attempts to get both legs over one side of the slippery lounger, he compromised and settled for one leg on either side. This was not a solution, however, as he found he did not have the strength in his legs to push himself into a standing position. The other loungers were quietly edging towards the dining room, and the prospect of being marooned across his sunbed while lunch was being devoured without him spurred our man into calling for help from his wife.

It was immediately obvious that whatever lifetime diet helped create the huge, rounded and wobbly magnificence that was Sun Lounger Man, it had been devised and supplied and shared by the lady now undulating, unappetisingly topless, by his side. Together they addressed the problem. From one side of the lounger, she grabbed her husband under the arms and heaved, upwards, several times. This failed because, a, the angle was wrong, b, she did not possess sufficient strength, and c, they were both oiled and slippery. It was like trying to wrestle an under-inflated bouncy castle.

Lunch was now very close to being served. People were drifting towards the dining room. Food was about to be eaten. This was not the time to be faint-hearted. Shining spectacularly in the lunchtime sunshine, Lounger Lady grabbed her hubby's left foot and yanked it, leg attached, over the lounger to join the other leg on one side of the bed. So much for the angle. Now for the test of strength. Facing each other, her feet braced in a weightlifter's clean-and-jerk, her arms round him, she eased her man forwards towards her, then, slowly, slowly, hoisted him to his feet. At the crucial point of this endeavour, and just before the pair reached tipping point and crashed backwards, the little strength in Sun Lounger Man's legs kicked in and like two enamoured sumo wrestlers, they quivered and wheezed their way upright.

I don't think they heard the round of applause from the *Benidorm* section of the pool. They were too busy scurrying towards their eagerly awaited and, in this case, well-deserved lunch.

Benidorm, 2009.

PLAYING CHICKEN

"Nuthin' could be easier. Fur a schoolmaster's son, ye can be affy dozent."

"Listen. Ye tak the matches, right? Ye set fire tae the damp grass where the eggs usually get laid fae the ootside, right? The smoke gings intae the hen hoose, and the first one that bangs on the door tae be let oot is chicken, right?"

Stuart Robertson nodded in agreement and took the matches from me. "Bluebell Scottish matches, average contents 47 matches," it said on the box. What a bargain! The fun you could have with 47 matches. With 47 matches, you could be the terror of the village.

Allan Campbell, the twinny Moirs – Ian and Jimmy – and I clambered into the empty, tiny henhouse. More for bantams than hens, really. "Right. Light up!" Stuart, the headmaster's son, would never have had the nerve to go into the henhouse, so he was given the job of getting the damp grass in the two-way laying boxes to smoulder and smoke, and stand guard at the door with instructions to unlock it when the smoke got too much for us.

We'd played this game of chicken in this real chicken house a million times before. Allan, the twinny Moirs and me would grab lungfuls of air as the smoke billowed into the wooden shed, then be reduced to pressing our mouths to the cracks in the floorboards in the final choking moments before one of us could take it no longer. The first one to bang on the inside of the door to demand release from Stuart would be declared chicken. Then the other three would explode out on to the grass after the chicken, sucking in the clean Scottish country air. Then we'd all recover and do it again.

We had a two-acre garden with fruit trees, vegetable garden and the hen run. We also had long summer holidays and parents who were very relaxed about seeing us only at mealtimes. We all went to Mr Robertson's Letham Primary School, and the village was our world. Our parents must have feared what we were up to. We'd come home for our tea stinking of smoke, or soaked in the burn, or covered in mud and almost certainly scratched or damaged in some way.

The chicken game was great while it lasted. Everyone had a chance to win, or not lose. It all depended on when you grabbed your last big breath of clean air and how quick you were thereafter in getting down to the cracks on the floor. The twinny Moirs were the postman's twin sons, Allan Campbell was the third son of John Campbell, the village policeman, and my Dad did something for the government. And all of us nearly didn't make it past ten years of age.

The choice of the grass for the smoking laying boxes was always crucial. Too damp, and it would just go out. Too dry, and, well, that must have been what happened on the last day of the game.

No one is blaming Stuart, the schoolmaster's son. He was only a wee boy, a shade more delicate than the rest of us, who was never keen on the three-fold responsibility of gauging the density of the smoke and the dryness of the grass, and being the keeper of the gate. So when he saw that the grass was not just smoking but that the whole side of the henhouse was smouldering alarmingly, he went home.

Inside, nobody noticed at first. Allan and I were still on our feet, while Ian and Jimmy had their mouths glued to the cracks in the floor. I think it was Jimmy who broke first. He banged on the door for Stuart to release us, but nothing happened. He banged again, and it was only then that we noticed it was not only smoky in there, it was very, very hot. No one was coming to open the door. The smoke was now evil and acrid and clothes were starting to singe in the heat. Four wee boys running around a tiny wooden shed in blind panic. So, with the strength that only panic can instil, the four wee boys stretched and heaved the roof up and off, and following Jimmy's inspired lead, we jumped blindly through the smoke to the grass outside.

Recovery took ages. We didn't spend much time pondering how close we'd come to death. That would come later. Our main discussion was how we could explain to our mothers why our clothes had become blackened and charred and were reeking of smoke, and why none of us had any eyebrows.

Letham, 1954.

LEG IN THE HOLE

It was a great little part, on paper. Homeless man, with dog, illegally kipping in a derelict warehouse, is accidentally blown up by a hitherto unexploded bomb. Whose bomb? Who knows? This is TV.

Long scenes of homeless man, now minus his right lower leg and trapped in wreckage, being rescued by firefighters and the staff of The Royal, the local hospital, and the name of the YTV series. The dog escapes unscathed. Then follows a happy ending scene in The Royal, when our hobo, now recovering, is touchingly, and illegally, reunited with his dog. Sunday evening television at its best.

The location was suitably grim, outside Leeds. Inside the wrecked warehouse the special effects team had dug a hole to receive my real right leg, bent from the knee, while costume and make-up contrived a very realistic stump. I knew I was going to be in this hole for some time, as the scripted rescue operation was difficult and painstaking. Coincidentally, a few months earlier, I had spent a couple of weekends learning the bewildering art of self-hypnosis, so I thought this would be a great opportunity to find out if it actually worked. Stuck in the hole for hours on end, I could tell myself I would suffer no discomfort from the location, the cramped position or the cold weather, and that I would remain calm, co-operative and uncomplaining through the long filming days.

And it was cold. Even with thermals on under the illegal dosser's rags, the cold soon gnawed down into the marrow. I was inserted into what was to be my home for the immediate future, and then covered with a blanket of charred beams, distorted corrugated iron, earth and plaster dust.

Setting up a shot takes time. The director, cameraman, camera operator, lighting designer, sound man, make-up lady, designer, prop man and special effects operatives all have to be satisfied. Then the director can flex his muscles with the cast, requesting, commanding, cajoling. Finally, realising that it's not going to get any better however long we try, he can then call: "Action!"

Reclining on my bed of dirt and rubble, I was well aware of how cold I was, but, amazingly, having "zapped" or used my recently-acquired self-hypnosis, I was actually very comfortable lying there, smug as a bug in a rug. Lights were tweaked, boom angles sorted, the stump was double-checked by make-up, costume and special effects, and off we went again: "Action!"

As the day wore on, I was aware of a different sensation. My hidden-away perfectly sound lower right leg and foot, tucked down its custom-built hole, had been cold, like the rest of me, all morning.

But now it was also WET. I pointed out this unscripted extra to the special-effects guys. With great care, with continuity in mind, they removed the charred beams and the distorted corrugated iron. A quick flash of a torch confirmed our fears: my hole was filling up with water. The director, unable for once to blame the actors for the hold-up, clasped his hands to his forehead and walked away. The assorted technical staff put their heads together and eventually came up with a solution: A WELLINGTON!

Another delay while wardrobe was summoned and the search ensued for a single wellington, size 9.5, right.

Back down the hole, foot dried, welly on and now protected, I added a self-hypnosis clause, protecting me from low water tables in the vicinity, and unforeseen wetness. The self-hypnosis held throughout the day. Tea and coffee breaks came and went, and I stayed in my hole. Leading actors from the series, handsome doctors and pretty nurses, turned up for their scenes beside the injured hobo, safe from the warmth and comfort of their Winnebago motorhome and moaning bitterly about the cold and the damp.

The director pointed out that I, a proper trouper, had been down that hole, uncomplaining, since the first shot, while they... I made few friends among the acting community that day.

Self-hypnosis was a smart move. I've used it subsequently to help me through an unexpected bout of stage fright, and as a painkiller. It has got me, you might say, out of many a hole...

Leeds, 2011.

THE CORPSING OF LORD FOPPINGTON

"Pssst!"

"Eh?"

"Pssst! Stuart!"

"What?"

"I can get you a goat!"

"What?"

"I can get you a goat!"

"A goat?"

"Yeah. I can get you one."

"What would I possibly want a goat for...?"

"To corpse Hugh. You remember..? To corpse Foppington."

Corpsing is one of the hazards of the performing arts. It can happen at any time, for any reason.

Originally thought to mean trying to make an actor on stage laugh when they are pretending to be dead (a corpse), corpsing now means any unintentional fit of the giggles in full view of a paying audience.

The goat was being suggested by stage management of the Leeds Playhouse production of Sir John Vanbrugh's *The Relapse, or Virtue in Danger*. It was to be our secret weapon to trap Hugh Ross, a notoriously disciplined actor playing Lord Foppington, into the biggest corpse of his career.

We were already halfway there. Our director had decided to give my character – Sir Tunbelly Clumsey – an enormous dog, a Pyrenean mountain dog, as an on-stage companion. It was a huge, shaggy, slobbery thing about the size of a mature Shetland pony and it ambled amiably after me both on and off stage. So the cast were livestock-aware, if nothing else.

"Where is this goat?" I asked stage management.

"On my brother's farm. I can bring it in tomorrow. We can hide it in wardrobe until it's needed."

We decided the goat should make its stage debut on the last night of the play, in the crucial scene when Sir Tunbelly, a rip-roaring, overweight country squire, meets the suitor to his daughter, the extravagantly attired man-about-town and fortune hunter, m'Lord Foppington. Normally, the huge and scruffy Sir Tunbelly would crash on to the stage accompanied by his pet hound from the Pyrenees on a lead, to be introduced to the exquisite Lord Foppington, all satins and lace and wig and with huge feathers in his hat. We reckoned Hugh would be at his most vulnerable then, having just arrived at Sir Tunbelly's country seat.

In a gap in the action, I left my canine companion in my dressing room and shot upstairs to wardrobe to greet the goat. I had the dog lead and collar with me, but they were to prove superfluous to needs. The goat was TINY. More of a kid, really. It was brown and white with beautiful eyes and two little down-covered horns. Change of plan. It was too small to lead onstage, so I swept it into my arms and prepared for our entrance.

The goat might have been small, but it was a trouper. The moment we stepped on stage, it started to bleat, loud and clear, enabling me to ad-lib: "Down, Rover! Down!" The audience went "Ahhhhh!" The unexpecting cast squealed and sniggered and some turned upstage, shoulders heaving.

Mr Ross was magnificent. He clocked the goat. His eyes widened in disbelief, he took a very deep breath, and just as I thought he was about to have hysterics, he swept his plumed hat off his be-wigged head and bent low into one of the longest, most flowery Restoration bows the British theatre has ever witnessed. Waving the feathery hat in one hand and a perfumed lace handkerchief in the other, he bent down over his be-ribboned knees and stayed there. He was corpsing all right. We could see him shaking. We could hear him laughing fit to choke, bent double. But no one in the audience would have guessed.

My goat was still bleating in my arms when Hugh eventually stood up straight, slightly red in the face but calm, in control, corpse-free, and triumphant. We had failed. The scene continued, goat and all.

Of course, there were repercussions. A very stiff letter from the director went up on the company noticeboard over the weekend, saying he'd never witnessed such unprofessional behaviour in all his years – three – as a director. We should all, especially the perpetrator, be thoroughly ashamed of ourselves, and if we wanted to discuss the episode further, his door would always be open.

The goat returned to his farm, probably boasting about his stage debut to the other farmyard animals. Our director was reduced to approaching the corpse-plotters in the next few days, inquiring if we wouldn't care to discuss our unprofessional behaviour. Nobody did. We had tried, and we had failed. Mr Ross's reputation remained intact.

Anyway, we were all too busy with our next and final play in the season, *Saved*, by Edward Bond.

Leeds, 1973.

BEING A BAIRN IN LETHAM

We were surrounded by fields in Letham, and our street, the aptly-named "Braehead", was on the outskirts of the village. Come winter, you could rely in those days on two or three heavy falls of snow. Every family with kids had a sledge, stored away most of the year, but first sighting of a snowflake... out they all came.

At the same time, seemingly without any planning, "Corrie" joined everyone at the top of the favoured sledging hill. No one ever knew where she came from; no one ever claimed her or took her home. Sometimes, almost by accident, she'd survive from one winter to the next, but usually she was too wrecked and rusted by then to be useful, so she was replaced. Corrie was a single sheet of corrugated iron, bent upwards at the front: a simple multi-passenger sledge capable of carrying up to six kids. Even fully loaded, she was fast, especially late in the afternoon when the temperature dropped and the run became icy.

The sledging hill was ideal. A flat loading area at the top of the run provided a starting point for the brave and foolhardy, with other joining stations further down for the younger and less courageous kids. The descent was suitably steep and scary, and the run-off required only a little caution. The only snag was the Vinney Burn. It meandered the full length of the bottom of the field, and was quite deep in places. There was nothing to stop an over-zealous tobogganer: no fence; no hedge. Just a two to three-foot-high bank, eroded here and there, then into the rheumatic winter flow of freezing burn water.

I have no recollection of ever seeing an adult on our sledging hill. The children were king.

My older brother Bill and his friends, in their early teens, were the only thing resembling a responsible adult. Close to the end of play for the day, this particular afternoon, with the light beginning to fade, Bill and Derek Mitchell and a squealing and giggling bunch of youngsters boarded Corrie at the top of the hill for one last run. Corrie had been busy all day and she and the slope were by now hard frozen. Helped by one final heave from a couple of the bigger boys, Corrie took off.

I don't know which of the younger children first decided that Corrie was going too fast, but I saw him roll off on to the hard snow. There was a pause, then another decided to bale out.

Corrie was now lighter. And faster.

Bill and Derek stayed on, perhaps because they were bigger boys and couldn't be seen to be afraid. The other smaller children quickly computed the speed of Corrie and the distance left to travel before the Vinney Burn became a problem, and regardless of the possible bruising, slipped off on to the icy snow. This left Bill and Derek hurtling at top Corrie speed towards what's known in that part of the world as "a dookin'".

Corrie left the field at maximum revs, but the action after that seemed to be in slow motion. Bill and Derek, still aboard Corrie, appeared to hover, momentarily, above the water, before slipping gently into it. By this time, however, their little legs had already started running on the spot to get them out. It just needed the Scooby Doo bongo running feet sound effect to accompany them both as they sprinted, as fast as their sodden trousers and legs would carry them, back up the bank and the hill. Ignoring their freezing, chafed legs, they scampered to the warmth and sanctuary of their respective homes and, inevitably, to a resounding telling-off from their scolding mothers.

Letham, 1953.

JIMMY PERRY AND THE CAMEL-HAIR COAT

"Good morning, everyone! Sorry I'm late. Discussions with my tailor took longer than I expected."

It was Jimmy. Jimmy Perry, our co-author, and we forgave him immediately because we knew that Jimmy's relationship with his tailor would be worth a few laughs in the first available break in rehearsals.

Jimmy, along with David Croft, who also produced, wrote *It Ain't Half Hot, Mum*. We tried for years to work out which scripts were Jimmy's, which David's, or even who had written which individual parts or lines, but we never could. Jimmy's writing career had been kick-started by *Dad's Army*, where, as an actor, he had taken the precaution of writing in a juicy part for himself. He had found himself in demand for brash, loud, wide-boy parts, so he created Private Walker, the company's black marketeer and spiv. Sadly, his co-author and producer, David Croft, pointed out that writing the show and being in it was not a good idea. Jealous fellow actors would accuse him of writing the best lines for himself, and so the notion was quietly shelved. In came James Beck, all pencil moustache and Cockney charm.

The curve of Jimmy's life and times was mirrored by the shows he wrote. While too young to join the army during World War Two, he helped out with his local Home Guard, giving us *Dad's Army*. When he was able to enlist, he found himself in Deolali Transit Camp, in central India, organising concert parties, which gave birth to our show. Demobbed, he became, among other things, a Butlin's redcoat, hence *Hi-De-Hi!*. He then recycled the talent from those three shows into *You Rang, M'Lord?*, the BBC's light-hearted reply to ITV's *Upstairs Downstairs*.

Sartorially, Jimmy was a star turn. Very showbusiness. Not flash, exactly, but certainly flamboyant. And effortlessly co-ordinated. He arrived that morning in what could only be described as a riot of autumnal hues. A variety of rich shades of brown in the check of the jacket, complete with the obligatory Water Rats lapel badge, on top of cream slacks above beige and brown two-tone brogues. The shirt was a dark burgundy with a discreetly striped Windsor-knotted club tie.

This was grist to the mill of Ken MacDonald, a Mancunian with a quick and, at times, merciless wit. He played Nobby, one of the hairy-arsed squaddies.

"Dear God! Look at that," he said, nodding in Jimmy's direction. "He's sat there like a fecking bowl of muesli!"

At the break, Ken asked Jimmy how things were with the tailor.

"Just grand," replied Jimmy.

"What's he making for you now?" inquired a suspiciously solicitous Nobby.

"Ah," said Jimmy. "A coat. A beautiful camel-hair coat. He's the best, but not the most expensive tailor in London."

Over the next few weeks, at Ken's prompting, Jimmy

kept us fully up to date with the coat's progress, until, finally, there it was, with Jimmy in it. He sashayed into the restaurant on the top floor of "the Acton Hilton", the BBC's six-storey rehearsal rooms in west London. It was, indeed, a very beautiful coat, if perhaps a little long for modern tastes. The weight of the material was impressive too; it hung beautifully, but with a certain chunkiness around the lapels, where the material had been doubled over.

The gang cheered the entrance. Especially Nobby.

"Is this it, Jimmy? Your camel-hair coat?" he inquired.

"This is it," replied a smiling Jimmy.

"Give us a twirl," said Nobby. Jimmy obliged.

"Beautiful. This is the coat you've had made by the best, but not the most expensive tailor in London?" continued Nobby.

"That's right," said Jimmy. "He's without doubt the best tailor in town, but he's certainly not the most expensive."

We watched, fascinated, as Jimmy walked into the trap.

"And this is genuine camel hair?" said Nobby, leaning forward to examine it more closely.

"Certainly," Jimmy replied. "Genuine hair from the belly of the Bactrian camel."

"Beautiful," said Nobby, gently fingering the chunky lapels. "But... Jimmy... surely..."

We waited.

"Should he not have taken the humps out first?"

London, 1979.

OLYMPIC HENDO, DEMON GYM MASTER

To our class of twelve-year olds at Forfar Academy, Olympic Hendo was an awesome sight. A former military PE instructor, Mr Henderson was built like a shoebox on legs. He had also been a boxer in the army and sported a seriously flattened nose and one very large ear and one normal-sized ear, presumably the result of having met other boxers from other regiments who were bigger and faster than him.

Why "Olympic"? No one knew for sure, and no one was brave enough to ask him. It was rumoured that when stationed in Asia with the British Army, he had been invited to coach the Thailand boxing team for the Olympics, or was it the Gurkhas? That rumour was never confirmed. He was our gym teacher, and a very good one. He at least was a character, unlike the customary assortment of anaemic sadists and shifty chain-smokers who constituted the younger male teaching fraternity.

Discipline was kept mainly by force of Olympic Hendo's personality, and when that failed, the belt. He never used it on me, but his speciality was to lay damp towels over the wrists of the offending pupils, so that only the hands were struck. Teachers in Scottish schools were permitted, almost encouraged, to hit their charges with the belt, the strap, the tawse. Three names for the same thing: a specially manufactured strip of leather about a metre long and forked – two prongs or three, according to taste, at one end. Teacher would clutch the un-forked end and bring the forked tongues of leather down sharply on to the outstretched hand of the pupil, up to six strokes – three on each hand – at a time. This was all bloody painful. And entirely legal.

New teachers were rated by the belt they brought. The worst, from a miscreant's point of view, was called a Lochgelly, named after the failed mining village in Fife where a cobbler first created it. A strap available in four different weights, which, correctly applied, hurt like hell. "He's got a Lochgelly", went the whisper, and the task of imposing discipline was already half done.

Lochgelly owner or not, Mr Henderson was, we discovered, ever so slightly accident-prone.

Once a week, our class would walk the half-mile to the local baths for swimming lessons. Our swimming pool was one of many such buildings donated around Britain earlier in the century by Dunfermline-born American steel magnate, multi-millionaire and philanthropist Andrew Carnegie.

Built of red sandstone, it was basic and functional, and always, even in the height of summer, freezing.

This particular day, Olympic Hendo announced he was going to demonstrate to us how to do an inward somersault on the springboard. We groaned. We knew from past experience that we were in for at least fifteen minutes standing shivering at the side of the pool, when all we wanted to do was mess about in the water. "Balance, boys, balance," said Mr Henderson through his squished nose – he always sounded as if he had a heavy cold as he stood facing inward at the end of the springboard, arms outstretched. "Balance. Watch."

He bounced up and down on the board, his voluminous ex-army cellular trunks flapping as he soared. "It's all about balance and control," he repeated, as with one deft, cushioning move the board steadied and was still again. The class shivered, thin arms across our chests in an attempt to retain some heat. Off he went again. "Balance and control, boys, balance and control." The board was complaining as Mr Henderson quickly reached optimum height and velocity. For a big man, he was almost graceful. He took off eventually, off and up and out. The inward somersault was executed. Up and over and out and down he went.

Unfortunately, not quite far enough out. The reverberating board clipped him on the way down.

It was only a slight, glancing blow, but it must have hurt like hell. Mr Henderson crashed into the water, sank, and fifteen little boys jumped in too to rescue him. In a maelstrom of splashing arms and legs, Mr Henderson was helped to the edge of the pool, dazed and glazed. He recovered some composure, and slowly refocused.

Shrugging off the unwelcome attention of his charges, he regained some more composure. "Ah, boys," he eventually said, gazing round and smiling unconvincingly. "What's a little bump on the head?" Too late. His image as one all-powerful supreme athlete had been irreparably dented, as had his head.

Weeks later, he repeated a land-based version of the same mishap. Every Thursday afternoon, our class would slouch over to the Strathmore Rugby Club ground on the shores of Forfar Loch. A marshy pitch, sometimes decorated with evidence of recently grazing cattle. Playing as coach and also stand-in full back, Mr Henderson had been shouting instructions and tactics to his class when he had to quickly back-track to catch a really good up-and-under kick from one of our better players. The height of the kick gave Mr Henderson time to yell the instruction "always keep your eyes on the ball, boys" and we all had time to anticipate the result as the ball descended.

Running backwards at speed, keeping his eye on the ball, he smacked straight into one of the posts, whacking it with all his considerable bulk and the back of his head. Down he slumped. The post was still reverberating when we got to him. "Are you all right, sir?" we inquired, then, considerately, "what's a little bump on the head, Mr Henderson, eh?" we chorused.

"Ah. Eh? What?" replied the dazed and glazed teacher. Then: "Oh. Yes. Of course. Quite."

Forfar, 1957.

THE TWO POUND BREASTS

Nigel Kneale scared the bejazus out of me. He terrified my Mum and Dad as well.

Two months after the biggest television audience this country had ever known – estimated at twenty million – for the Coronation of Queen Elizabeth in Westminster Abbey, viewers were back in the same location to watch a huge dangly mutation of an infected spaceman who had returned to earth threaten the Abbey, London, and the entire planet. *The Quatermass Experiment* was the first television science fiction we had come across. There were six spooky weekly episodes on the BBC – then the only television channel in the country – and the nation was transfixed. Happily, Professor Bernard Quatermass was on hand to save us all. Nigel Kneale wrote *The Quatermass Experiment*. He followed this up with *Quatermass and the Pit*, equally popular and even more scary,

So it was with great pleasure that in 1972, some nineteen years later, I was told I'd been cast in *Beasts*, six single plays by Mr Kneale, this time for Lew Grade's Associated Television. My play was called *Buddyboy*, the tale of murky goings-on at a London dolphinarium.

Perhaps difficult to believe now, but a dolphinarium, underground, was opened in 1971 in Oxford Street, London, on the site of a defunct cinema, by a company called Pleasurama. Audiences were entertained by the tricks of two dolphins, Bonnie and Clyde.

Mr Kneale, in *Buddyboy*, opens in a dolphinarium that has gone bust following the unexplained and suspicious death of the lead dolphin, Buddyboy. The owner of a cinema showing porn movies – played by Martin Shaw – is thinking of buying it to expand his empire. I play his cinema manager.

The plot says I have persuaded one of my usherettes that I can get her out of selling ice cream and tissues and into the glamorous world of pornographic movies. To aid her career, I have suggested she pops into the office to strip for my boss.

We record at the ATV Studios in Elstree. Somehow, word gets out that a well-endowed young lady is going to disrobe. Now, every studio has a complement of different trades on hand to minimise expensive delays should anything go wrong on set. Approaching the disrobing scene, though, there was an extraordinary and exponential multiplication of painters, electricians, stage hands, carpenters, security personnel and casual passers-by, wielding brushes, screwdrivers, hammers, saws, clipboards, anything to legitimise their presence. However, the sudden arrival of a curious, multi-tasking audience made the girl playing the usherette, a stripper from Brighton, very nervous. She explained that it was quite easy to be revealed semi-naked at the end of an exotic dance routine to music on a stage in a club, but cold stripping, as required in this scene, made her nervous and uncomfortable. Martin, gentleman that he is, insisted the set be cleared. Much harrumphing and shuffling followed, but then we got down to rehearse and record. Halfway through a discussion about the proposed change of use for the dolphinarium in my office, the well-endowed usherette enters. "Shall I do it now?" she asks. I nod. Then she does, quickly removing her blouse to expose her talents.

"Very nice," says Martin casually. "Now get back to work."

To cover the embarrassment as she leaves, I ask my boss: "D'you know how much they weigh?"

"What? Weigh?" says Martin. "You weighed them?"

"Ay. Two pounds apiece," I reply. "We were fooling around with the kitchen scales at her mother's!"

Thank you, Mr Kneale. Actors kill for lines like that. One take.

The owner of the dolphinarium was played by Wolfe Morris, guilt-ridden and nervously sweating throughout as he could be implicated in the unexplained death of Buddyboy. One morning, he arrived on set in a grand old state, fizzingly angry at something or other. First chance, I asked him if he was all right. "You won't believe this," he spluttered. "I was running late this morning. Too late for my train from Hampstead to the studio. So I hailed a black cab. The cabbie was courtesy itself, until I told him I wanted to go to Elstree."

"Elstree? he said. Then, erm, sorry, mate, I have a fare.

"He obviously didn't fancy a longish trip to Elstree. Listen, I said, in the first place, I am not your mate, and secondly, I have hailed you, and by accepting, under the terms of the Hackney Carriages Act, you are obliged to take me to any reasonable destination in the Greater London area without equivocation. Do you understand?"

"He rolled his window right down, and looking me squarely in the eye, he said, Bollocks!

"I was outraged. I informed him that I would report his behaviour and intransigence to the appropriate authority to have his licence revoked as he was in contravention of the aforementioned Hackney Carriages Act. Looking chastened, he performed a quick three-point turn, ending up pointing towards Elstree.

"I was about to get in as he pulled up beside me. Instead, he rolled his window right down and said, Double Bollocks. Mate. And he sped off!"

"I swear I saw him smirk as he left. This country's going to the dogs."

London, 1972.

WHAT, TREVOR, YOU MEAN... SPEAK?

At twenty-four years of age, after three years as a journalist and three years at drama school, I started my second acting job – spear carrying with the Royal Shakespeare Company in Stratford-upon-Avon. Trevor Nunn, only four years older than me, was beginning his first year as artistic director of the whole shebang.

I was in all five plays of the season: *King Lear* (Soldier, Riotous Lord, French Attendant, Soldier again), *As You Like It* (Exiled Lord in the Forest of Arden, Deer Slayer), *Dr Faustus* (Devil, Monk, Gatekeeper to Hell), *Troilus and Cressida* (Emblem Bearer, Soldier – both armies, Trojan and Greek), and *Much Ado About Nothing* (Soldier, Dirge Singer and Messenger). Rehearsals for the next show during the day and eight performances a week, including matinees, kept all the spear carriers busy. Not that there was much to do in Stratford anyway.

There were other excitements, though.

Michael Williams, playing the Fool in *Lear*, wrenched his ankle playing football one Sunday morning. His understudy, Bruce Myers, had disappeared off to the Lake District for a couple of days and was uncontactable. It was quite early in the run, and our tight schedule meant we had only had one or two understudy rehearsals, and the Fool is a pig of a part to learn and play, full of puns, word plays and gags that we all suspected were unfunny in Shakespeare's time, never mind 1968. So poor Bruce wandered into the theatre half an hour before curtain up on the Monday evening, only to be told he was going on for Mike Williams. True to the traditional and ancient theatre edict that the show must go on, Bruce's first reaction was to exclaim: "Cancel it!"

He went on, though, bravely, and mightily assisted by the riotous lords and spear carriers, who had been at all the rehearsals and knew most of the words. Any time Bruce was in danger of floundering, he'd invoke the help of a lord or two. "Ah, nuncle, nuncle," he'd exclaim, banging his tambourine and capering up to a spear-carrying knight, fear in his eyes... And the knight would give him the clue, and off he'd go again. Mercifully, Shakespeare kills off the Fool halfway through – "And my poor Fool is hanged" – so Bruce was able to get off and lie down in a darkened room to recover.

I worked with Bruce years later, and when I mentioned to him light-heartedly that he'd supplied me with one of the most memorable moments in all my time in the business – meaning his blind panic on being told that he going on as the Fool – he blithely replied: "Ah yes. *The Dybbuk*!" Bruce had recently played the lead in *The Dybbuk* by Shloyme Zanvl Rappoport, aka S Ansky, at the Almeida Theatre in north London. And he seriously believed I was referring to that. I let it go...

Anyway, Mr Nunn's busy year included directing *Much Ado about Nothing*, the final play of the season. Terrific cast, led by Janet Suzman and Alan Howard.

Saturday morning in the rehearsal room, on schedule, Mr Nunn was nailing the last scene of the play. "Right, Stuart," he said. "I want you to come in top right over there, cross down left here to Norman, and give him the line."

"Eh?"

"That's right. Enter top right, cross to Norman who is sitting downstage left, and give him the message."

"The message?"

"Yes, Stuart. The message. See? Here? The message. 'My Lord, your brother John is ta'en in flight and brought with armed men back to Messina'."

Now, this was the fifth and last play of the season, and the penultimate line of the last play of the season, and I was a spear carrier. In all the previous eight months and four productions (see above), no one had ever asked me to actually speak.

"I'm not sure," I said. "You mean, cross to Norman" – the inimitable and charming Norman Rodway, impeccably playing Don Pedro – "and give him this message?" A slight sigh from Trevor, a man long used to discoursing with idiots, then: "Yes. Stuart. Exactly."

"What, Trevor? You mean, speak?"

"What?"

"You want me to speak to Norman? I mean, say the line? 'Your brother John is ta'en in flight and brought with armed men..?' That line? Speak? I'm not sure, Trevor. It's been eight months. Speak?"

It took a moment, but then I felt the surprisingly firm grip of Mr Nunn's hand on my right arm. The eyes narrowed, the lips and the grip tightened, and the usually equable Mr Nunn hissed: "GET UP THERE. Stuart. NOW!"

The play opened to excellent reviews. Justifiably. As well as Suzman, Howard and Rodway, the cast boasted the incomparable double act of David Waller and Clifford Rose as Dogberry and Verges, Terence Hardiman as Don John, who, as you now know, was "ta'en in flight and brought with armed men", etc, etc.

Ben Kingsley, now Sir, and Patrick Stewart, now also Sir, were Don John's henchmen and fellow baddies, Conrade and Borachio, and Sebastian Shaw was Leonato. The reviewers, probably for reasons of space, oddly made no mention of the virtuoso performance by the messenger right at the end of the play. Which was a pity, because I thought he was really rather good.

Stratford-upon-Avon, 1968.

TEAS VISOCCHI'S ICES

ANGELS IN KIRRIE

Some images never leave you. Given the particular and precise ingredients of time, of place, of receptivity, of shock and wonderment, some pictures take up permanent residence, never to be dislodged.

Kirriemuir on a teeming wet Saturday morning is depressing. Red sandstone can look handsome in sunshine, but dulls in the inky reflection of the sodden pavements and black tarred roads. Grey and cloudy above, dank and gloomy below.

Miserably plodding from the square to the newspaper shop set back from the road, I turned the corner and there they were: three angels, veiled, clad in white dresses which illuminated the whole street, dark-haired, each holding a bouquet of white flowers. Angels in Kirriemuir, breathtakingly beautiful. I see them now.

Of course, there was an explanation. The Visocchi girls, and, I think, a cousin, on their way to confirmation. But just for a moment, as the image nestled into my consciousness, there were angels in Kirriemuir.

MY ONE AND ONLY HONEY SHOW

In my first year as a beekeeper, thanks to my beekeeping guru and friend Richard Palmer, I actually had honey in jars. I had successfully hired the centrifugal extractor from the local association, de-capped both sides of the frames, and slipped them, three at a time, into the extractor. Turning the handle on top, I heard for the first time the most beautiful sound in a beekeeper's world: the hissing, sizzling sound of honey spinning free out of the uncapped comb on to the inner walls of the extractor. A tap at the bottom of the extractor, a final sieve to collect the tinier pieces of wax, and there's your honey, unadulterated, organic, straight into the jar.

I was so thrilled that I decided to enter my honey in the novice class of the forthcoming Surrey Beekeepers Association, Croydon Division, Honey Show. I followed the strict instructions. The honey had to be exhibited in clear, traditional one-pound squat jars of British Standard pattern, with standard lacquered lids. It should be filled precisely, with no visible gap between the top of the honey and the bottom of the lid.

I dropped off my entry, entry fee and entry form and left the judges to it.

Besides my novice class, there were many different

classes, for clear honey, light, medium or dark, honey in the comb, set honey, chunk honey, honey cake, honey chutney, and a separate section for "two beeswax candles, one of which will be lit”. So later that afternoon I returned to discover my honey's fate. There, among all the other entries from really experienced beekeepers, was my novice first attempt. In front of my jar was a blue ticket announcing to the world that I had won second prize! And next to that was a small brown envelope containing my prize – a 50 pence coin.

I was delighted. Second prize at my first show.

A dapper wee man appeared at my elbow as I was packing my honey away. He introduced himself to me. He, apparently, was the judge who had awarded me second prize.

"I suppose you want to know," he said, "why you were second."

"Oh, I don't know," I said loftily. "Anyway, how many entries were there?"

"Two," he said.

"Ah. All right then," I said, "why was I second"?

He leant forward conspiratorially. He glanced left and right before murmuring: " Bubbles."

"Eh?"

"Bubbles," he repeated. "There were bubbles."

"Is that bad?" I asked.

"Ohhh," he said, sucking his breath in between his teeth and shaking his head sadly, "you won't win anything with bubbles in your entry. You'll always be second. Or worse."

"Actually," I said, "I'm not all that both..."

"Have a look at all the other entries. Experienced beekeepers. Not a bubble anywhere."

He clasped me by the elbow and came closer. Lowering his voice, he asked: "How do they do it?"

"How?" I whispered back.

Resuming normal volume, my newly appointed bubble authority said: "You take the top off the jar, and place the jar in a pan of warm water. The heat makes the bubbles eventually rise to the surface."

"With you so far," I said, wondering if I'd ever get home.

"Then you take a teaspoon and guide the bottom of it over the surface of the honey. The bubbles will adhere to the teaspoon and then you can dispose of them."

I was amazed. "How long does this take?" I inquired.

"Depends how many bubbles you've got," came the reply.

"Well, thank you," I said, "but I really do think that life is too short to spend any of it de-bubbling honey." He stepped back, stunned. It was as if I'd hit him across the face with a freshly caught haddock.

"I... What..? You..," he stammered.

"Sorry," I added. "I'm very grateful, but this is just a hobby."

"Right," he said. "Fine. If that's what you think..." And with a despairing shake of the head, he turned towards the stage and his next duty, the prizegiving.

My day was completed when just before I left we were treated to a brief lecture from the wife of the honey judge, who was an expert on making things from beeswax and whose task was to judge the entries in the "two beeswax candles, one of which will be lit" section. In a very powerful voice, she opened her judgment by declaring: "I've told you all time and again, and time and again you ignore one of the basic laws of beeswax candlemaking, which is 'Always, always remember to wipe your wicks!"

As I was the only one laughing, I thought it best that I pick up my honey, bubbles and all, and leave.

Croydon, 2014.

TOM JONES AND THE PUTTY NOSE

Repertory theatre in the provinces was where a young actor learned his craft. To land a rep job for a six-month season, on a "play as cast" contract, left little time for anything else, which was just as well, because the money you earned wouldn't pay the admission into anywhere else.

Most theatres by the time I was released from drama college were running three-weekly seasons, but some were still putting on a new show every two weeks. The actor's nightmare, and it happened from time to time, would be to suddenly launch into the wrong play on the wrong night.

Our season at the Flora Robson Playhouse in Jesmond, Newcastle upon Tyne, included works from Arnold Wesker, Christopher Marlowe, local boy James Mitchell, and an adaptation of Henry Fielding's *Tom Jones*. I was heavily into experimenting with different make-up at the time, and when asked to play Tom's sadistic teacher Thwackum, I decided a hooked, beaked nose – for a beak – would be appropriate. I invested in a lump of mortician's wax. Before every show I would painstakingly tidy up the wax and mould it into a slim and malignant proboscis on top of my own small characterless appendage. Playing Thwackum obviously involved a lot of cane-swishing, and pursuing the delinquent Tom Jones around the stage. One very warm evening, in the middle of this action and in mid-swish, dashing in pursuit of Tom, the putty nose and I parted company. I knew it had gone, and remarkably, with my free left hand, I caught it on the way down. In one flowing movement, I smacked it back on to my face, much to the horror of David Cook, the engaging young actor playing Tom. I failed to realise that an aquiline, sculpted nose, detached from the face, would bear little resemblance to one hastily shoved back on. Tom and the rest of the audience saw the nose was no longer slim and sadistic, but squashed and grotesque. I resembled one of these strange fish that are regularly discovered in the deeper and darker reaches of the ocean.

Word of this mishap quickly got back to the director, whose advice was, bluntly, to "pack it in", and leave the application of mortician's wax, in future, to morticians.

Newcastle upon Tyne, 1970.

THE DUNDEE COURIER AND ADVERTISER

Where I was brought up, the *Dundee Courier and Advertiser* was like the Bible. Everybody believed every word in it. Both testaments. If it's in the *Courier*, it must be true.

Its format tried to emulate its prestigious cousin in London, *The Times*. A broadsheet, it had all the small ads on the front page, with local and national news, social gossip and sport, and most importantly of all, yesterday's livestock, fish and potato market prices inside. The paper was owned by a family firm, DC Thomson, which also published the *Dandy* and the *Beano* – Desperate Dan, Dennis the Menace, Lord Snooty and his Pals, and the Bash Street Kids – and a library of weekly magazines for girls. The editorial line reflected the readership: solidly right-wing, respectful of authority, the Empire, the Kirk and the Union, and at the same time virulently anti-trades union. It was, to put it mildly, up itself.

If the *Daily Express* had the William Hickey society column, detailing the scandals and peccadilloes of the country's most upper of the upper classes, the *Dundee Courier and Advertiser* could boast Fiona's Column. Although the area was replete with lords, ladies and earls in their country estates, their activities went unreported by Fiona, who instead had to make do with lesser mortals, like the wife of the commander of RAF Leuchars, or the Dean of Guild on the Forfar Town Council. I disliked the *Courier,* for all the reasons mentioned above.

One fine morning, when travelling to work at the *Herald* in Kirriemuir, I was intrigued to see DC Thomson delivery vans belting round the narrow country roads like rats in a maze. Willie Ogilvy, my boss, could hardly contain himself. Bruce Prophet, the Linotype operator, and Ally Bruce the apprentice printer were also wearing unfamiliar grins for that time in the morning.

"Have ye seen this?" roared Willie, before I had time to ask him about the vans. "Have a look at this. Un-be-bloody-lievable. Look!"

He spread out that morning's *Courier and Advertiser* on the stone and waved at the small ads on the front page.

"What am I looking for?"

"There, man," shouted Willie, and jabbed an inky finger at the Hotel and Catering section of the Jobs Vacant column. "Look there! There!"

I looked.

"Willing, experienced barman required," it read.

"Please apply to:
Miss Mary Likes,
The Cockwell Inn,
Tillit,
Wilts."

Oh my God! In the *Courier*! Bloody hell!

That would explain the DC Thomson vans spreading all over the county like lichen. They were trying to get the offending papers back. Eventually, all of the east of Scotland was in on the rude advert and either tut-tutting or sniggering. Repercussions at the paper were swift and remorseless. Anyone remotely connected to the advert, copytakers, proofreaders, printers, stone subs, small ad salesmen and women found themselves outside, clutching their P45s. Remember, this was a non-union shop.

The *Courier* never fully recovered from the scandal. It's true that the more po-faced and self-observing you are, the more profound the loss of face when the edifice is breached. After Miss Mary had told the readership what she liked, it was impossible to truly trust anything in the *Dundee Courier and Advertiser.*

Kirriemuir, 1960.

HILP, HILP, OH HILP!

So. The army of Lear's good daughter, Cordelia, has been defeated, and she and Lear have been taken off to prison. His other daughters, Regan and Goneril, are fighting for the attention of the mega baddy, "God, stand up for bastards" Edmund. The victorious army, led by a sympathetic Lord Albany, husband of Goneril, piles on stage to celebrate their victory and establish the new order, when dreadful news is brought on stage by a distraught messenger.

Among the spear carriers in the Royal Shakespeare Company in Stratford-upon-Avon, there was serious competition for the crumbs from the top table, the tiny speaking parts of serfs, messengers, and assorted casual hangers-on. The part of the vital messenger at this crucial juncture of *King Lear* had been entrusted to one Robert Oates, a keen and valued member of the spear carrying fraternity.

Like many of us, Bob's training had embraced the carelessly defined "method" school of acting, which demanded complete involvement and submersion in any part, however tiny. His job here was to launch himself on stage carrying a bloodied dagger, crying "Help, help, Oh help!" and bearing the shocking news that Goneril is dead, poisoned by her jealous sister

Regan, who has then, in a fit of remorse, stabbed herself in the heart. Bob would warm up for this in the wings, bouncing up and down on the spot with his back to the stage before turning on cue and making his entrance. It might have been the effort required, but by the time Bob got on stage, the cry of horror came across not as "Help, help Oh help", but more like "Hilp, Hilp, Oh Hilp".

Bob's swivel and snap turn was very effective, and he launched himself onstage at a rate of knots, but this particular performance was well into the season, and other plays had featured for months on the same space. One of these was Marlowe's *Dr Faustus*, which involved a scene where the pope and his candle-carrying monks in the Vatican are baited by Faustus-inspired demons. This had led to a build-up of spilt candle-wax on the stage floor, waiting, we were soon to discover, for Mr Oates's entrance. Bob's cue came. In the wings he bounced, the offending bloodied dagger in hand, turned and ran on.

"Hilp, hilp, Oh hilp!" he hollered. Everyone turned, just in time see Bob slip on the wax, land on his arse, and slide inelegantly past an astonished Albany and his entire army diagonally across stage, coming to rest with a painfully loud "whump!" against the downstage left proscenium arch.

There was a stunned silence.

Terence Hardiman as Albany and Norman Rodway as Edmund, not surprisingly, took a moment or two and a few deep breaths to recover. The surrounding army, less disciplined, hid its sniggering face behind shields, spears, hats, anything it could find. One or two soldiers just gave in altogether and turned upstage, shoulders heaving. The audience had already been watching for nearly four hours, so didn't have the energy to work out whether or not this was part of the production.

Bob, still clutching the bloodied dagger, disentangled himself from the pros arch, and, trouper that he was, continued magnificently with the scene in spite of the suppressed mirth assailing him from all sides. Into this then walks the distraught Lear, cradling his hanged, dead daughter Cordelia in his arms.

Eric Porter could tell something was up from the very first of the five "howls" he has to scream on his entrance. A fleeting expression of inquisitiveness passed over his features, and then he set to work on recovering the scene, and the play. No one, his face told us, was going to jeopardise the immense amount of hard bloody work he had put in over the past four hours.

In subsequent performances, though, we all noticed that Bob's entrance was slightly less exuberant, so from then until the end of that season the proscenium arch was free of his attentions.

Stratford-upon-Avon, 1968.

THE PLAY SCHOOL YEARS: K'TOO

Cockatoos are very noisy birds. I discovered this on television. Each week on *Play School,* one day was devoted to the pets. There was a glamorous two-tier run full of white mice, a couple of rabbits, goldfish, etc, etc. Now and again, an animal would die and have to be replaced, and a presenter, usually the more sympathetic female presenter, would gently explain the pet's non-appearance to the impressionable pre-school viewers.

The star of Pets Day was K'too, a magnificent sulphur-crested cockatoo. She – I always assumed it was a she – was a particular favourite of the viewers and the pride and joy of Wendy Duggan and her husband Ron, the minders who looked after her and all the other pets. Although she was beautiful to look at, K'too was a pain to work with. No discipline. Without warning, she would emit a series of the most ear-achingly painful screeches, right across whatever story, song, or sticky-tape creation was in progress.

"Hello, everyone," the presenter would say at the top of the show. "Do you know what..."

"Scrrrrraaaaack!" would go K'too, nodding her head

and flashing her crest in the background. "Scrrraaaaaaack!"

"Yes, K'too," the presenter would ad-lib, acidly, "it's a..."

"Scraaaaaack..." Another flash of the bright yellow crest, a triumphant "Up yours!" to the studio.

We tolerated this – she was, after all, the star of Pets Day – until I made a chance discovery with a mop. On the set was a small, miniature mop of the kind used in the kitchen for washing dishes. Pets Day was just about to record. The floor manager started to count me in.

I had the mop in my hand for the first item, and casually waved it in the direction of the screeching K'too, muttering "shurrup" under my breath. The response was immediate and astonishing. K'too went into a kind of stunned, blinking trance, her head tipped questioningly to one side, her crest flat and unfurled on the top of her head. It only lasted a few seconds, but it was completely effective. She was silent and I got on with the programme.

So, from then on, obviously, any time I saw the crest twitch and K'too started winding up for a disruptive screech, a quick wave of the mop would traumatise her into silence. And I soon discovered that the longer the mop was waved in front of her beak, the longer she remained immobile and absolutely quiet. It wasn't something to boast about, but I soon earned the gratitude of the entire studio, especially the sound recordists.

Until one day, Wendy, the pet lady, caught me at it. She was livid. She was a big woman, and usually friendly, calm and affable. Not this time. She gave me the most monumental bollocking. All about how sensitive these exotic creatures were, how they bravely survived in an alien captive environment, and how I had probably taken years off the bird's life by thoughtlessly and cruelly frightening it into silence.

It was a much-chastened presenter who got on with the rest of Pets Day after that.

Fast forward twenty-five years. I am attending Wendy's funeral in Putney. Among the many speakers at the service, paying tribute to Wendy's professionalism, kindness and fierce protection of her beloved pets, was the king of all the *Play School* presenters, Brian Cant. During a memorable eulogy, Brian mentioned that he had visited Wendy at home shortly before her death, "and there by her side," he said, "as noisy as ever, was K'too".

I was surprised and delighted. So much for taking years off its life! Twenty-five years of guilt wiped out in a sentence. As far as I know, K'too is alive and well and still screeching. She will probably outlive us all.

London, 1978.

THE SCOTTISH DAILY MAIL

My introduction to the offices of the *Scottish Daily Mail* in Edinburgh – my new employer –could have been handled more diplomatically. As I had no idea where I was or where the offices were when I arrived in Waverley station, Edinburgh, I grandly hailed a cab and instructed him, importantly, to take me to "the *Daily Mail* offices". Eventually he drew up, down a side street, at what looked like a works entrance.

"The front door, please," I said, expecting an imposing, modern, glass-fronted building worthy of a national newspaper. "The front door!"

"This is the fuckin' front door," said the cabbie, and it was to be my home for the next few months.

The *Forfar Dispatch* and the *Aberdeen Evening Express* had both decided I was not God's gift to journalism, but the *Scottish Daily Mail,* ignoring history, had decided to take a chance that I was perhaps a late developer. I was still hankering after an actor's life, and the *Scottish Daily Mail* supplied the impetus to take me there.

I have always maintained that if you have a dream you have yet to pursue, then opening the door into that sub-editors' office would give anyone courage. First, none of the subs wanted to be there. Everyone had other ambitions: the great Scottish novel, sheep farming in the

Cairngorms, a B and B in Rothesay, anything... The top desk, with the chief sub, the copytaster, etc had a good superannuated reason for being there, but the subs?

Retirement drinks were another motivator. Across the road from us was Marshall's Bar, where we would congregate in the evening meal break. It was a horseshoe-shaped bar, and when someone from the desk came up for retirement, somehow, mysteriously, the subs managed to arrange themselves around the bar in order of seniority. Anyone recently in would be at the bottom of one leg of the horseshoe. Round at the other end, the retiree would position himself to accept the drinks coming his way. So you could see your own future, as your gaze panned round the bar. Did you really want this?

I decided I didn't.

The City editor was a gentle soul called Ray. Well into middle age, he favoured a hairstyle dictated by having very long hair round the sides of his head but, sadly, none on the top. Ray's comb-over was carefully crafted in the gents toilet downstairs before every shift and meticulously maintained throughout the evening.

I had decided, given all the hints mentioned above, to apply to the Royal Scottish College of Dramatic Art for an audition. Success would mean a three-year course in acting, the first step in what might even be a career. I had passed the audition some three years earlier, when my father decided, very wisely, not to finance this experiment. Hence the drift into journalism.

Ray came into the office for the first edition, hair in place and ready to go. I collared him at his desk and told him I had decided to leave the *Scottish Daily Mail* to try to become an actor. His eyes widened and he grabbed the lapels of my jacket in both hands and shook me.

"Do it," he shouted, his eyes going like catherine wheels. "Fucking do it!"

His carefully coiffed hair, now disturbed, cascaded back down on to his shoulders, exposing a shiny, slightly sweaty scalp. He stomped off, still agitated, back to the gents toilet.

"All right, Ray, I will. I'll try my best," I replied, limply, to his retreating figure. "Honest. I will."

Edinburgh, 1963.

OH, WHAT A LOVELY WAR!

John Harrison's inaugural season as director of the Leeds Playhouse in 1972 kicked off with Bertolt Brecht's *Caucasian Chalk Circle,* followed by *Oh, What a Lovely War,* by Charles Chilton. I was cast as Simon Chachava in the Brecht play, a gift of a part for any actor. Simon turns up in the first few scenes, woos and wins Grusha, the feisty heroine. He then goes off to war, with everyone remembering him fondly and missing him terribly, and he eventually pops up near the end of the play to behave heroically and to be reunited with his long-lost girlfriend.

Lots of brownie points for very little effort. As I say, a gift of a part.

As I was so little required in rehearsals, and I was anxious to help, I volunteered my services to Mr Harrison to help whip up publicity for the plays and for the theatre. I quoted my previous career as a journalist, and a trifle unwillingly, and with my promise that I would run everything past him, John gave me the go-ahead.

I concentrated on our second show, *Oh, What a Lovely War,* and came up with a corker of an idea to help publicise it. The play is set in an end-of-the-pier theatre, and through song and dance tells the story of the astonishing heroism and murderous folly of World War One. Originally written by Charles Chilton, *Oh, What A Lovely War* was first presented by Joan Littlewood and her ensemble at the Theatre Royal, Stratford, in the east end of London.

My corker of an idea was simple. Why not invite 100 veterans of the First World War – remember, this was 1972, and there were still many survivors – and give them an afternoon out at the theatre?

I got in touch with the local Royal British Legion, who said they would find the veterans, and the Leeds Taxi Drivers Association, who promised to ferry them to the theatre and back home for free.

Then I told John.

Come the day, the Saturday matinee, our regular audience was boosted by 100 former soldiers, some wearing their medals, with their wives and long-time Royal British Legion supporters. Joan Littlewood's production had the end-of-pier show populated by pierrettes and pierrots – attractive girls and boys who sang and danced – being presided over by a master of ceremonies, who introduces the acts, and sometimes in this show, scenes from the horror and carnage of the war, interspersed with songs of the time. On paper, it sounds clumsy and awkward. On stage, it is alternately funny and desperately moving.

All went according to script up to the interval. Almost immediately after, though, there is a pantomime singalong, with the audience split in two, one half singing *It's a Long Way to Tipperary*, the other *Pack Up Your Troubles in Your Old Kitbag*, each side being encouraged to compete and sing up by the MC and the pierrettes and pierrots. As we got to the end of the singalong, a little silver-haired lady walked out of the audience in the stalls, up the two steps and on to the stage.

"I would like to sing you a song," she announced.

John Rainer, our master of ceremonies, was momentarily flummoxed, but then stood to one side.

Annie – as we all came to know her later – simply said: "I'd like to thank the theatre, and the boys and girls for putting on this wonderful show for us."

She then sang, beautifully, *Bless This House*. At the end, there was silence, and not a dry eye in the house, or on stage. The happy-go-lucky singing-and-dancing all eyes-and-teeth pierrettes and pierrotts were incapable of continuing. Mascara was running everywhere...

At this point, a very tall, ramrod straight-backed man made his way on to the stage. He towered over little Annie and announced: "I'll sing you a song." And added pointedly, looking down at Annie: "On me own!" He then sang a very rude song about officers, which none of us knew, but all the veterans in the audience did. A couple of choruses and we all got the show back on track, to a warm and happy conclusion.

Tea was laid on for our guests, and the cast joined in to hear stories of the war they were portraying, but had never experienced.

"We were known as the Five Loonies," said our straight-backed soloist from earlier. "We all came from t'same street. Once, there were this injured Jerry out in no man's land, screamin' his 'ead off for hours. I told me mates 'I can't stand this. I'm goin' to gerrim'. It's dusk, so I reckon I can have 'im back wi'out bein' seen. When I got to 'im, he were shouting in Jerry an' pointin' to where 'is leg shoulda been. It 'ad been blowed off. So I sling 'im over me shoulder, 'is head down me back, and stagger back to our side. 'Alfway home, there's this bloody huge bang right close, bloody muck and shrapnel everywhere, blew me off me feet. I held on to 'im, though, and staggered on till I got back to our trench. Me mates gathered round, then said 'What 'ave ye brought 'im back for? 'Is 'ead's been blowed off'. I 'ad a look. It 'ad. Must've been that last bang.

"Jus' goes to show," I said. "You can't trust the bloody Jerries. 'E told me it were 'is leg!"

Teatime for the veterans ran on into the half-hour warning to cast and crew for the evening performance. Nobody moved. We were all enjoying the company of our guests and their reminiscences. They were enjoying the food. The Leeds Playhouse at that time had a well-deserved reputation for heart-stopping – literally – cakes and huge sweet pies and puddings with lashings of double and clotted cream. It was rumoured you could feel your arteries harden while just standing buying tickets at the box office, one floor below the cafe.

The matinee guests and the evening performance audience and the cast, still in full costume and make-up, made it a memorable and unique afternoon tea. The Leeds taxi drivers were patience personified, waiting until the last of our guests was ready to go home, and we returned to the stage for the evening performance, rewarded and enriched by an unforgettable afternoon that had started out as a simple publicity stunt.

There was an added bonus. The *Yorkshire Evening Post* reported the event, and a reader, who had not seen the show, wrote to the paper's letters column complaining at this "tasteless" gesture, having the veterans relive their wartime experiences. The response was terrific. Many of our veteran friends wrote to the paper, saying what a grand afternoon they had spent, and thanking the cast for so thoroughly entertaining them.

We played to very good houses. Then it was back to more serious business.

Our next show was *Macbeth*.

Leeds, 1972.

THE PLAY SCHOOL YEARS: MR PRINGLE

"Quiet, please, studio," said the floor manager. "We've gone as far as ... QUIET!!!!" The entire studio rattled briefly after the second shout.

I had long believed that floor managers at the BBC TV's floor manager school were given special voice-projection classes, especially the women. They had two voices. One cool, calm, soft, gently urging the technicians and actors to progress smoothly from one scene to the next. The other, the one we had just heard, could sear the skin off your cochlea at twenty paces.

"That's better," said our floor manager, back in Voice One. "We're moving on."

We were recording *Play School*. It was always a hectic schedule: five twenty-minute programmes rehearsed in one day and then recorded – two on Monday, two on Tuesday, the last on Wednesday, for transmitting Monday to Friday the following week. This one was to be different. We were to be introduced to Mr Pringle.

"We've gone as far as we can," said the floor manager. "All that's left is the song and dance with Mr Pringle. Can we call Mr Pringle, please?"

The assistant floor manager made for the studio door, hidden behind the cyclorama. We heard the door open. I glanced at my fellow presenter, the assured, the unflappable Carol Leader. Even she looked a little tense. We could hear a footstep, an almost sinister footstep, a slide and thump to every pace. Cameramen, sound recordists, lighting men, sparks, assistants, even assistants' assistants waited. Then he appeared round the corner of the cyclorama with his keeper.

Mr Pringle, a beautiful king penguin from Chessington Zoo.

One of the joys of *Play School* was that you never knew what you'd be asked to do next, and with what. The scriptwriter, who on *Play School* was usually also the director, could come up with any number of bizarre ideas, and if they were within budget and mildly educational – and obviously the hire of a penguin was – then the strange idea became a reality. So there we were, scripted to explain a bit about king penguins, where they came from, what they ate ... and then finish with a song and dance.

Mr Pringle was very tall and dignified. If he felt out of his comfort zone in a BBC television studio, he didn't show it. He was probably less flustered than I, trying to remember all the scripted interesting facts about him and his relations in Antarctica.

After the educational bit, I had to say "I wonder if he's hungry?" and present him with a recently dead mackerel.

Nothing. I dangled the fish in front of Mr Pringle. He looked straight ahead, his shiny eyes fixed keenly into the middle distance. I tapped him on the head with it, hoping to interest him in a quick snack. Still nothing.

"Cut!" said the floor manager, back on Voice Two. "Why," she inquired of Mr Pringle's keeper, "isn't he eating the fish? Weren't you asked to make sure he was hungry?" "He's very hungry," replied Mr Pringle's keeper. "Trouble is, he's been hand-reared, and only recognises food if you slide it in at the corner of his beak."

The floor manager's eyes lifted briefly heaven-ward. She could be doing the Classic Serial or the Play For Today, for Godssake! Instead..?

"Right," she said with a kind of sigh. "We'll try that. Pick up the fish, Stuart. Quiet studio. And, action."

"Penguins love fish," I ad-libbed furiously as I tried to get a decent grasp of the mackerel. I poked the fish head towards the corner of Mr Pringle's beak. "I wonder if he's hungr... ooyah!"

I counted my fingers. All there. But of the fish, no sign. It had vanished like lightning down the bird's gullet the moment the head touched the beak. So he was hungry, after all. There was a beat of a second, and then we all discovered something really interesting about penguins – if not penguins in general, certainly about this one in particular. The moment it eats, it craps.

In one end and out the other. There, on the studio floor.

Now, jobs at the BBC were much sought-after. Get in at an early age on the lowest rung and who knows? Director-general or beyond. Look at Esther Rantzen, former junior assistant floor manager, now national treasure. Our assistant floor manager that day was a refined, gentle young soul called Adrian. Whatever arduous and complex obstacles he had expected to face in his rise up the greasy career pole at the British Broadcasting Corporation, picking up penguin shit was obviously not one of them. An unconcerned Mr Pringle was gently moved to one side, and Adrian, utterly unable to conceal his appalled disgust, swamped the offending and malodorous discharge into a huge bale of paper towels, en route to the bin. We then made our second exclusively penguin-related discovery of the day. Penguin poo lifts studio floor paint. We were now in danger of seriously over-running the time allotted to recording the final *Play School* of the week, but the painter was duly called to repair the damage, a heater was brought on to try to dry the new paint and off we went again.

"Quiet, studio," said the floor manager soothingly, now into damage limitation mode. "We'll pick it up at the song." Carol and I had rehearsed a pleasant little ditty along the lines of a penguin being a funny bird, being unable to fly but being very fond of fish. It wasn't a classic, but it rounded the item off nicely. Trouble was, no one had rehearsed Mr Pringle. He just stood there next to the drying patch of new paint, aloof and uninterested.

The director in the control room spoke to the floor manager and the floor manager spoke to me. "Can't you persuade him to move about a bit? He's very static."

I was about to explain that the mobility of penguins was not something I was an expert in, when Mr Pringle's keeper sidled up. "If you want him to move," he whispered conspiratorially, "knee him in the back of the head."

"What?"

"Yeah," the keeper added, this time tapping the side of his nose knowingly, "The back of the head. With your knee. It's what I do."

"Right, studio. We're running out of time," said the floor manager. "Quick as you can. Ready, Carol? Ready,

Stuart? And action. Go music." There then followed a triumphant three minutes of television, incorporating the combined skills of our musicians, the director, the vision mixer and the two performers. Briefly, there were three cameras, one close up on me, one close up on Carol, and one taking a wider shot of Mr Pringle and our legs. A light at the front of the camera indicated which shot was being employed and accepted by the vision mixer.

The music started, and when I was sure the camera for Carol's close-up was on, I followed the keeper's advice and kneed Mr Pringle sharply in the back of the head. He lurched forward, in time to be caught by the wide-shot camera, and to all intents he looked like he was moving to the music.

"The penguin is a funny bird," we sang. Bop! And off went Mr P.

"He lives in the cold, cold sea" Bop! Off he went again. Wide shot, all three of us, then...

Close-up on Carol, then round behind Mr Pringle and Bop!

Off he lurched again, "He's not very good at flying," we continued, and a close-up on Carol, so Bop! again, back to first positions,

"But he loves eating fish for his tea," we sang triumphantly.

A bemused Mr Pringle was glancing from side to side. He looked like he was really enjoying himself. The song came to an end and the studio went quiet. A moment to check what we'd just done. "Thank you, studio," said a relieved floor manager in Voice One. "That's a wrap!"

London, 1978.

"AH'M GONNY BE AN ACTOR, SIR!"

"And what do you want to be when you grow up?" asked Mr Crampsey, the history teacher. I'd been asked this a million times before by assorted fond aunts and friends and relations, and I was mmediately on my guard. The question had got me into trouble before.

To move from your primary school to senior school, all children of my age, in the day, as they say now, you had to sit an iniquitous exam called the eleven-plus. The outcome could change your life. Fail the eleven-plus and you'd go to the local senior secondary school, and if you were lucky, start to learn a trade, somewhere to use your hands, not your brain, because the exam had demonstrated you didn't possess a brain big enough. Pass the exam, and in my part of the world, you'd go to an academy – in this case, Forfar Academy, in the county of Angus on the east coast of Scotland, with the offer of a classical education: French, Latin, German, Greek even.

The eleven-plus was a glorified aptitude test, the methodology shaky and subsequently thoroughly discredited, an exam that hurt children and split families. My big brother Jim passed, my second brother Bill didn't. I passed, my younger sister Margaret didn't.

I was very worried about the exam because the love of my life, the beautiful tall, dark and willowy eleven-year-old Joan Litt from my village of Letham, was very brainy and was sure to progress to the Academy.

It might not have been part of the exam, but I distinctly remember being asked: "What do you want to be when you grow up?" I was ten. (I went to school at four, a year early, not because I was outstandingly gifted, but because my mother, with my little sister to look after, wanted me out of the house asap. I was, apparently, a particularly energetic and reckless child.)

So, prior to the eleven-plus exam, when I was asked the grown up question, I had a quick, mercenary think. "Who's rich? Who lives in a big house, has a great job in a suit, not an overall? Most important, who has a flash new car every time I see him?

"I want to be a doctor," I announced to my astonished parents. "Ay, that's it. A doctor, when I grow up!" My Mum and Dad made the imaginative leap from seeing this smudged, scruffy, snot-encrusted oik of a son transformed into a revered professional pillar of the medical establishment and the community within seconds, and thereafter, whenever I was asked what I wanted to be when I grew up, my mother would answer for me. "A doctor."

It took ten years and my departure to drama school to eventually disabuse my parents of their ambition to have a doctor for a son. I had sadly chosen the wrong theatre to operate in. So when Mr Crampsey, the new, young and charismatic history teacher, went round our newly-formed class, one at a time, asking the grown-up question, I decided to be brave.

"AH"M GONNY BE AN ACTOR, SIR!" I squeaked

defiantly. Mr Crampsey raised an eyebrow and waited for the storm of sniggers from my classmates to subside. He had just the suggestion of a smile himself as he took the information on board. Where can this child have got this bizarre idea from? The third boy of a family of farmers, the father now working for the Ministry of Agriculture, the mother the daughter of a farmer, no connection whatsoever with the theatre, and he wants to be an actor? Mr Crampsey accepted the information, and, as I discovered later, filed it away for future use.

It was exciting to have him teach us, as the grapevine quickly discovered he'd once been the goalkeeper for Queens Park Strollers, the second team of one of Scotland's oldest football clubs, still all-amateur, who played at Hampden Park, the country's international venue. He also went on to win BBC Radio's *Brain of Britain*.

Fast forward twenty years and I'm due to record a half-hour play for BBC TV at Pebble Mill studios in Birmingham. Signing in, I notice one of the Beeb's visitors is a certain Mr Robert Crampsey, now a renowned Scottish author, football commentator and journalist, visiting to talk about his most recent book about the city of Glasgow on *Pebble Mill at One*, a daily magazine programme. Come lunchtime, and I seek him out in hospitality. He's still charismatic, charming and handsome. He remembers me because of my odd and unexpected declaration that morning in Forfar Academy. He adds, enigmatically, that he had been able to discover the fortunes of another pupil, Felicity.

Felicity was a tall girl, the daughter of a Forfar vet. She walked as if she'd had ballet lessons, and wore her hair in a long, single plait that reached down to her waist. All of this made her look rather aloof, like a Thelwell pony club member cartoon. "When I asked Felicity the grown-up question," said Mr Crampsey, "she replied 'I'm going to be a member of the Queen Alexandra's Royal Army Nursing Corps, sir'. That was the second surprise of the morning, you being the first.

"I've seen you on television, of course, so I know you fulfilled your ambition. And a few years ago, I was reading – I don't know why – the engagements column in my *Glasgow Herald*. There it was: parents "delighted to announce the engagement of their daughter Felicity, QARANC, to..."

"So, you and Felicity, eh?" said Mr Crampsey. "Well done."

Birmingham, 1980.

DR FAUSTUS NIL, BILLINGHAM 1

In October 1969, the Flora Robson Playhouse in Newcastle upon Tyne did a culture swap with the Forum Theatre, Billingham, 50 kilometres down the Northumberland coast. Billingham took our production of Christopher Marlowe's *Tragical History of Dr Faustus* and, in return, Newcastle got the Forum's production of *Billy Liar,* by Keith Waterhouse and Willis Hall.

Peter Gordon, a notable Royal Shakespeare Company associate artist came to Newcastle to give his Faustus, and I played Wagner, his manservant. The Forum was a curious space to play. A comparatively new theatre, it had spurned the fashion of the day towards a more egalitarian "theatre-going experience" and had been built with old-fashioned boxes. We were told later that the town was virtually owned by the chemicals conglomerate ICI, and the boxes were for the company's well-heeled senior executives and their wives. It also doubled as a cinema, which we were soon to discover.

The Faustus plot is straightforward. Faustus, a scholar and doctor from Wittenberg University, Germany, sells his soul to the devil, Lucifer, and in exchange he is granted extraordinary magical powers, and untold wisdom and wealth through Lucifer's sidekicks, Mephistopheles and Beelzebub. The first half of the play covers Faustus's renunciation of God, several lofty debates with Mephistopheles on matters theological, and his pact with the devil, written, of course, in his own blood, quickly, before it coagulates.

It's hard work. A tough, lung-stretching hour for the actor playing Faustus, all aimed at creating the mood, spirit and historical accuracy of the language and the setting. The act ended, in our production, on Faustus's visit to the Vatican, where, invisible, he wreaks havoc among the pope and his clerics. There's lots of slapstick and pratfalls.

We all returned to our dressing rooms: Faustus, Mephistopheles, the pope, assorted cardinals, archbishops, bishops and monks. Kettles were switched on, bottles opened, cigarettes lit, costumes loosened, wigs removed, the feeling of a good job, well done.

Into this, over the Tannoy blasted: "I'M THE KING OF THE JUNGLE, A JUNGLE VIP."

Followed by: "WHOOP DEE DO, AH WANNA BE LIKE YOU HOO HOO."

And then: "THE BEAR NECESSITIES, THE SIMPLE BEAR NECESSITIES..."

We gazed at the Tannoy speakers in blank amazement. Then it dawned. They were trailing next week's movie on the safety curtain.

Peter – Faustus – was the first to speak. "Fuck me!" he muttered.

Then, after a deep breath, "I've just spent the last hour trying to recreate the illusion of the world of 12th-century Wittenberg in all its profound, historical, ecumenical complexities. And then what do I get?

"YOO HOO HOO, AH WANNA BE LIKE YOU HOO HOO."

Head down on his dressing room table, he quietly muttered: "Give me strength."

Billingham, 1969.

OOYAH!

When I was very small, we were visited by a friend of my Dad's. He had come down from his farm in Morayshire to compete in the Scottish Beekeepers' Association's annual exhibition, being held, that year, in Dundee. As well as entering his honey in the various classes, he had also made figurines of moulded beeswax. They were beautiful and fascinating, even to a snotty-nosed ragged-arsed scruffy wee boy. These figurines, of various animals, birds, insects were left with us after the show, and turned up in the back of drawers and in cupboards for years afterwards.

Perhaps it was his farmer friend's influence, because several years later, my Dad decided to take up beekeeping on his own. Already in the village were two or three beekeepers, always willing to help and advise. Our hives were at the foot of a three-acre orchard and garden, and every so often my Dad would plod down to work at them. I've subsequently learned that you don't actually "keep" bees. You serve them, trying to anticipate their needs, and they can be very needy.

The regulation image of the beekeeper is a figure clad from head to toe in a bee-proof outfit – usually white – complete with face mask and smoker in hand, on his way to combine with some of God's most mysterious creatures to produce a mutually beneficial harvest. Not my Dad. He had the official hat with a veil tucked tightly into the neck of his shirt, and the smoker, and that was it. The sleeves of his jacket and the gloves were bee-proofed with elastic bands around the wrists, his trousers similarly secured with a combination of elastic bands and cycle clips. Bees, especially angry bees, are adept at finding tiny gaps in any human's defences, and my Dad had maybe ten to fifteen minutes before they worked out the weak spots. Sadly, most jobs took upwards of half an hour.

We kids would be playing round the house, usually with other children in the late afternoon or early evening when my Dad would make his way towards the hives, clad in his beekeeper's hat and veil, the smoker smoking furiously as he made his way stiffly, because of the elastic bands and cycle clips, down to the hives. All games ceased as the children found the best and safest places to watch from. We could see him lift the roof of the hive, the buzzing murmur of the bees growing in pitch and intensity as they realised they were about to be burgled. The smoker worked at full pelt to distract them.

The theory is that the bees, smelling the smoke, believe a fire is imminent, so consume as much honey as they can for flight to escape. A big meal of honey also fills and distends their bellies, making it more difficult for them to lower the sting into its target. That's the theory. In practice, it seemed to us that the smoker just made the bees mad as hell, and more determined to sting my Dad.

Working like fury on the job in hand, my Dad sensed

time was running out. That made him work faster, and, as a consequence, clumsier.

From our grandstand seats, the kids could hear Dad's breathing quicken, followed by familiar expletives as the bees worked their way past his defences. "Ohtaefu..!" he would exclaim, smiting himself on his wrist, followed by "Achyabast..," as another one got him in the ankle. If he heard the giggles in the distance coming from the assorted children in his audience, my Dad didn't pay any attention to them. He was too busy trying to get the lid back on the hive. By this time, all his defences had been breached and the angry insects were now inside his makeshift outfit.

My Dad was not an athletic man, being of stocky build, but he took off up the garden at great speed, clearing fences and obstacles like an Olympian, at the same time ripping off his bee-infested clothes and slapping at his persecutors. He was chased all the way up the garden and through the house until he could go no further. There he stood, breathless, in our bedroom, wearing his underpants and one sock, his body covered in red blotches caused by the stings and the self-inflicted violence.

Only then did he realise that not only his children, but all the neighbours' children had witnessed his astonishing performance and we're now gazing at him, grinning and giggling from the other side of the bedroom window. He was not a happy man. He later refused point-blank to attend to the bees in front of an audience, explaining that he could tolerate the pain of the stings, but not the embarrassment of the sniggering kids.

Letham, 1954.

PAUL SCOFIELD, A GENT

Early in 1972, I was asked by John Harrison to join the cast of his Leeds Playhouse production of *The Tempest* on its transfer into London's West End, with John's long-time friend Paul Scofield playing Prospero. I was less than thrilled by the part offered, Francisco, a minor nobleman. John's problem was that the part was so tiny that it had originally been played in Leeds by an Equity probationer, but the rules said that only full members of Equity could play the West End, and I qualified. In fact, in one copy of the play, a footnote observed that the part was probably not written by Shakespeare anyway and was usually cut. So John thought of me.

Briefly, through his magical powers, Prospero, the exiled Duke of Milan, conjures up a storm to sink a ship containing his usurping brother Antonio, and Alonso, the King of Naples, and the court on their way home from a wedding in Carthage. The beached courtiers, including Francisco (usually cut) try to persuade the shipwrecked king that his son Ferdinand has survived the tempest, "buffeting the waves with his lusty sinews". Mollified that his son is safe somewhere on the island, the king and his entourage, after a heavy night's buffeting, succumb to sleep. This being Shakespeare, however, no sooner has most of the court fallen asleep than the usurping Duke of Milan starts plotting the downfall of the King of Naples with the king's gullible brother Sebastian. *Plus ca change...*

After pages of debate, Sebastian is convinced. With their swords drawn, he and Antonio advance with malice aforethought on the sleeping king, only to be thwarted by Prospero's fairy attendant, Ariel. "Awake, Lords, awake!" cries the ever-watchful sprite, rousing the sleeping courtiers to the defence of their threatened lord. And that's where my troubles started.

On this matinee day, along with a few of the smaller-part players, drink had been taken at lunchtime prior to the afternoon performance. This was not an unusual practice back in the day. Then, all forms of the entertainment industry, be it theatre, film or television, were powered by copious quantities of alcohol, taken before, after, and sometimes even during performances. All changed now, of course. So when it came to falling asleep on the stage after the shipwreck, on a warm Wednesday afternoon in Wyndham's Theatre, it was all too easy to do just that.

"Awake, Lords, awake," screamed a demented Ariel, and all the lords did, except me. I slept on. I was awakened by a kindly fellow courtier kicking me in the head. I scrambled to my feet and drew my sword, but too late. Everyone knew. Even the audience knew. Genuinely asleep on the job. I was mortified. The rest of the show was spent suffering the sniggers and smirks of the junior members of the company and the disapproving glares of my more senior colleagues.

My only consolation was that Paul Scofield was not on stage to witness my somnambulistic lack of professionalism. Between shows, I stayed away from the pub. Come the evening performance, there was no courtier more determined to stay awake until Ariel ordered us to "Awake!" than Francisco, written by Shakespeare or not. Which makes what happened next even more difficult to explain.

I can only appeal to the motorists among you, who have experienced that split second of jerking panic while driving, tired, on the motorway. For that tiny moment, your eyes drop, and your worst and first fears are realised. You have fallen asleep, in spite of all your best efforts not to, and chaos and carnage will most certainly ensue. Then, in that same instant, normality returns, eyes open, driving resumes, and you promise yourself a break as soon as possible.

So it was with me on the stage. I believed that, in spite of my best efforts, I had fallen asleep again. I was determined there was to be no repeat of that afternoon's debacle, and so with great abandon I leapt to my feet, sword unsheathed, to protect my king against his unscrupulous brother and the plotters.

UNFORTUNATELY, A PAGE AND A HALF TOO EARLY!

I was the only courtier standing. The plotters, who had hardly had time to start plotting, looked up at me in amazement. One of them mouthed, upstage: "What the f*** are you doing?"

I quickly calculated what had happened. The next problem was, stood there awkwardly, how to extricate myself from this embarrassing predicament? And then my three years of intensive training at the Royal Scottish College of Drama kicked in. I know, I thought. I'll pretend I've had a bad dream!

So, if the plotters and the audience were bemused

and perplexed by my early arrival in the scene, they were even more astonished at my brazen departure. I yawned hugely, re-sheathed the sword, stretched mightily, gave a little shake of the head (classic bad dream recovery acting) and subsided slowly back on to the stage, utterly mortified. A page and a half later, Ariel told us all to awake in the right place, and we did, safely, and dead on cue.

I never discovered whether Mr Scofield ever knew or was told that I'd screwed up twice on the same day in the same scene, but if he did, he never mentioned it.

A real gent.

London, 1972 .

SOMETHING TESTICULAR

In 1989, I realised another ambition, though in very unusual circumstances. The climax of *Tutti Frutti,* the end of the Fabulous Majestics' less than earth-shattering Silver Jubilee Tour, came when our lead guitarist Vinnie Diver immolated himself in front of a disbelieving audience. The venue was Glasgow's Pavilion Theatre. Years later, a call from the Pavilion. Could I do them a favour? In the middle of rehearsals for the pantomime *Robin Hood,* the actor playing Little John had been taken off to hospital, suffering from "something testicular".

Maurice Roëves, who had played Vinnie in *Tutti Frutti* and was rehearsing the baddie Sheriff of Nottingham, had suggested I might be willing to stand in for the recovering Little John for the last couple of weeks of rehearsal and maybe a few weeks of performance. I jumped at the chance. Scottish pantomimes, and especially Glasgow pantomimes, are renowned. The audiences are vocal and demanding. The performances have to be at full throttle. It's broad brush-strokes time. No prisoners are taken. Panto has influenced Scottish acting style for years. If I had a fiver for every time a south-of-the-border director has said "Fine, Stuart. Could you just take it down a bit..?", I could have retired a lot earlier than I did. So going to

Glasgow on this errand of mercy was a no-brainer. Andy Cameron was our lead star, with a cast of well-known performers. Maurice, never one to duck a challenge, had grabbed the part of the villainous sheriff by the throat and was roundly booed by our packed audiences. The curtain call was a revelation. After we had all sashayed downstage in our sparkly walk-down costumes to generous applause, Mr Cameron then had the task of going along the front row individually for a bonus round. I was mentioned and thanked for standing in at short notice for the indisposed original Little John.

One matinee, at the final curtain, a little boy stationed himself halfway down the central aisle and proceeded to give Mr Cameron what can only be described as the dead-eye. He couldn't have been more than nine or ten years old, but he stood there in a boxer's pose, left leg forward, with his hands, fists clenched, by his side. His air of mini-menace was compounded by a pair of shorts and a vest, or semmit.

Andy was going through his re-introduction of the lead actors, but his attention was drawn back to this wee boy, or wean, and the concentrated malice of his pose. No one could devise what was going through this young man's mind. Andy was completely unnerved, and eventually asked anxiously: "Can I help you, son?" There was no response from the boy, but with a final, powerful dead-eye glare, he turned back up the aisle, sandals, shorts and semmit disappearing into the darkness of the rear stalls.

After a couple of very happy weeks playing Little John, the original Little John, now fully recovered, returned to the show. Apart from the "something testicular" diagnosis, no further mention was made of his temporary incapacity. Until one evening, when he was shadowing me to learn what we had rehearsed, I overhead him explain to one of the stage hands: "Ah'm tellin' ye, man. The size o' a lemon!"

I refrained from inquiring further.

Glasgow, 1989.

THE BARBER

He came to the village every Wednesday afternoon on the bus from Arbroath. We never found out if someone from the village had suggested this weekly pilgrimage to him, or if he was acting on his own initiative, saw the opportunity, and took it. More likely, it was, as he himself said, "to stop me from wearying". He opened up in the ground-floor room in the village hall in the square. One chair, two mirrors, a bench for waiting customers, and our village had its own barber.

He was a dapper wee man, the barber, neat and trimmed in the best traditions of his trade. The speak was he'd had his own business, had retired, and become bored. He was welcomed in the village. Up to then, you had to take a bus to Forfar, five miles away, to get a haircut, and like everything in Forfar, it was not cheap. Our barber had one fixed fee for bairns: sixpence. He also had one fixed style: closely shorn three-quarters of the way up your head, leaving an unruly, tufty clump at the top. Adults got the same treatment, until everyone from our village could be easily identified by our hair. There was no need to tell anyone in the county where you came from; they already knew by looking at the top of your head.

Every so often, the mothers would conspire to get all

their boys done at the same time. We all had to suffer the same difficult choice. Sixpences clutched in our grubby little hands, we all had to walk past Ecky Low's corner sweetie and ice cream shop. Ecky Low made the best ice cream. Only vanilla flavour – none of your fancy strawberry or chocolate or rum 'n' raisin – but it was the best ice cream in the county. On Saturday afternoons, the square would be packed with people out for a wee drive, ending up with a treat, a sixpenny cone or a chocolate slider from Ecky Low's.

That temptation safely negotiated, we'd sit in a row on the bench at the barber's, legs swinging, watching the man at work. It was like watching a harvester reaping a field of corn on a steep hill. The clipper would start above one ear and methodically work its way up and down, up and down, round to above the other one. A quick tidy-up of the top of the head and round the ears, then: "Next!"

This Wednesday, the barber was halfway round Mike Kerr's head when Jimmy Lindsay came bustling in. Jimmy, or Mr Lindsay as he preferred to be known, was the village postmaster, a very important role befitting a very important wee man. Jimmy was also known, behind his back, as "Provost" Lindsay. The village was far too small to have a provost, but that didn't stop Mr Lindsay from behaving like one. He frightened me, because one of my chores was to collect the Family Allowance from the Post Office every two weeks. I'd peer over the counter, hand up the Family Allowance book, and wait. As there were four in our family, it took a lot of checking. Mr Lindsay scrutinised every word of the document, glared at me suspiciously over his glasses, then slowly and reluctantly counted out the money. Every note was rustled and rubbed to within an inch of its life, Mr Lindsay apparently terrified that two notes could be stuck together, his calculations would be wrong, and he would give out too much money. The coins, likewise, were double-checked and the whole sum triple-checked before I was allowed to have it. This was all very embarrassing to a wee boy, who thought this was some kind of charity, paid only to poor people.

"Quick, barber," spluttered Mr Lindsay. "Ah've got tae catch the half past three bus tae Forfar, an' Ah was kept busy in the shop. Could you gie us a quick trim?"

The barber hesitated. He already had a customer in the chair.

"Ah have tae be there," explained Mr Lindsey. "It's an affy important meetin' o' the County Cooncil." He might not have been a provost, but he was every inch the county councillor. The barber decided. "Right, son, out ye get," he said, and a half-shorn Mike Kerr was eased out of the chair. "Wait there," he added, indicating the bench. Mike ignored him and legged it out of the shop.

"The usual?" asked the barber, apparently under the mistaken belief that he offered differing haircuts to different people.

"Aye," said the Provost. "Ah have tae look smart. It's an affy important meeting." The barber set to work. He had almost circumnavigated the Provost's head with the clippers when the door burst open. A tearful Mike Kerr was propelled into the room, followed by an absolutely fizzing angry Mrs Kerr.

"WHAT is the meaning of this?" she demanded, pointing at her son's half-finished haircut.

Mrs Kerr was English. Apart from speaking funny,

she was generally quiet, kind and considerate. She knew all the boys because she took the money at the door of the winter cinema showings in the village hall each Saturday night. Her husband Ron, Mike's Dad, was chief screen putter-up and taker-down. Mrs Kerr, we thought, wouldn't say boo to a goose.

All that obviously changed when Mike had run home with half his head shaved. She gave the barber what for, and once she discovered the part Provost Lindsay had played in the affair, he was given the very rough edge of her English tongue, using words we were not supposed to know the meaning of. Poor Jimmy tried to explain how important his haircut was, but Mike's Mum was now in full flow and would not be deflected.

The Provost was about to be hoiked out of the chair by an incandescent Mrs Kerr when the Forfar bus came to his rescue by chugging into the square. In spite of protests from the barber that he hadn't finished, Jimmy was out of the door, into the square and on to the bus with an agility that belied both his age and his girth. Mike was returned to his rightful place in the chair, and under Mrs Kerr's watchful gaze, his haircut was completed.

The affair had taken its toll on the barber, however, and after brushing down Mike, he declared he was closing and catching the early bus back to Arbroath. He would be there next week, he told us, but he needed to go home now. The rest of us managed to overcome our disappointment by spending our haircut money in Ecky Low's on the way home, knowing that the tale we had to tell when we got home was well worth the sixpence.

Letham, 1957.

IT AIN'T HALF HOT, MUM

I was called to the Acton Hilton late in 1972 to meet David Croft and Jimmy Perry, who were planning a follow-up series to *Dad's Army*. The Acton Hilton, or the Fun Factory, was a seven- storey block across the road from the Tube station in North Acton, north west London. The ground floor was for admin, the top floor, with balcony, housed the restaurant, and the other five floors were custom-built rehearsal rooms for all of the BBC's drama and variety output. One level even had a sprung floor for dancers. It was a great place for an actor to work in, to see and be seen.

Everything was rehearsed there. You could chat to the leading actors on the Classic Serial or Play for Today, or the dancers from *Top of the Pops*. I once saw comedian Russ Abbott in a serious head-to-head conversation with Sir John Gielgud.

It was a Monday morning, the only time I could get down to London from Leeds, where I was in the Playhouse company, playing eight shows a week. David and Jimmy were rehearsing the latest series of *Dad's Army,* while planning the next one, the continuing story of Jimmy's army career, *It Ain't Half Hot, Mum.* "IAHHM" was to be set in Deolali Transit Camp in Maharashtra state in western India at the end of the war in Europe. I was aware of *Dad's Army* earlier than most because Ian Lavender, who memorably went on to create the gormless Private Pike, and I were in the same company in Canterbury. It was his first job out of the Bristol Old Vic School, and mine, out of Glasgow. Ian's agent was David Croft's wife Anne, and at the end of that season he went off straight into *Dad's*. Five or six years later, it was my turn to sit opposite Messrs Croft and Perry and be quizzed. The Croft/Perry combo is one of the glories of British television comedy. Their careers and exploits have been well documented elsewhere, so I hope they'll forgive me when I say I returned to Leeds that afternoon, happy to have met them, of course, but especially thrilled to be introduced to a hero of mine and fellow Scot, John Laurie.

Mr Laurie, aka Private Fraser, the Walmington-on-Sea undertaker, was born in Dumfries in 1897, and was one of the most famous Shakespearean actors of his age. Of *Dad's Army*, he was once quoted as saying: "I've played every part in Shakespeare, I was considered to have been the finest Hamlet of the 1920s and I had retired, and now I'm famous for doing this crap!" He loomed over our table in the Fun Factory restaurant, stuck out a hand to me, a fellow Scot, and with eyes flashing announced: "They're all scared of me, y'know!"

I could well believe it.

Coincidentally, I was in Dumfries, rehearsing a *Play Away* outside broadcast, when news of Mr Laurie's death, at the aged of eighty-three, came through to sadden the whole town.

I knew there would be a problem doing the pilot episode of "IAHHM" because I was contracted to Leeds Playhouse. We were giving our *Oh, What a Lovely War,* followed by *Macbeth*. Then, with the touch of serendipity that seemed to follow me around, I was asked by David and Jimmy to play Gunner Atlas Mackintosh, and the week-long rehearsals and recording fell right into the middle of a ten-day break I had from the theatre when the children's Christmas show opened.

My first line in the pilot established the tone for Gunner Mackintosh.

"Sorry, Sergeant Major. Ah'm no' well. Ah've got the Bombay trots!"

To which the SM replied: "Have you been eating bananas without cutting the ends off first? Depot Orders clearly state Other Ranks will not eat bananas without cutting the ends off!"

Mackintosh was the strongman act in an army concert party, who along with their captain and colonel and Indian servants, were very anxious not to go "Up the jungle" to fight in the war. Sergeant Major Williams, the inimitable Windsor Davies, was dedicated to having the concert party disbanded, and its members made into "proper soldiers".

I was never called upon to do any strongman acting in the role, which was just as well. Reference was made to my ability to tear telephone books in half and to bend iron bars, but happily I was never asked to demonstrate this. My usual role was as chorus back-up to our leading lady Bombadier Beaumont, aka Melvyn Hayes, in his many drag roles on stage, and as a butch foil to his campery off-stage.

The part of the sergeant major was originally offered to Leonard Rossiter, who was wowing the nation in *Rising Damp*, but he turned it down. He was, according to Jimmy, not particularly complimentary about the script, either. It eventually came to Windsor Davies, who initially tried it as a Londoner, which didn't work. He was then invited to play it in his native Welsh accent and – Eureka! – Windsor was a revelation. He made the sergeant major "a part to tear a cat in". Michael Bates was a shoo-in for the part of Rangi Ram, the concert party bearer. He was born in Jhansi, Uttar Pradesh, India, and learned Hindi before English. He was also a very fine comedy actor, already successful on TV in *The Last Of The Summer Wine*.

The colonel and captain of the concert party, Donald Hewlett and Michael Knowles, established a formidable comedy double act from the pilot episode onwards. The slight distinction in class – upper versus upper middle – was beautifully written, and meticulously observed. In the pilot, and for the first two series, our corporal concert party director was played by George Layton, aka Bombardier "Solly" Solomons. He departed to continue a successful writing and acting career. Melvyn Hayes brightened the set up as "Gloria" Beaumont, the exceedingly excitable leading lady. This left the concert party made up of Londoner Chris Mitchell, as Parky, who was possibly the sergeant major's illegitimate son, the product of a brief liaison in Colchester.

Kenneth MacDonald played Nobby Clark, in real life the son of Bill MacDonald, Scottish heavyweight wrestling champion. He came from Manchester, and went on to play the pub landlord in *Only Fools and Horses* for many years. Mike Kinsey, from Birmingham, played Nosher Evans, the concert party paper tearer, always eating and spreading crumbs and bun shrapnel everywhere. Don Estelle played "Lofty" Sugden.

Described in one episode as "the singing coconut", Don was five foot nothing and almost spherical, but possessed the most beautiful tenor singing voice. In 1975, he and Windsor recorded the Ink Spots' *Whispering Grass*, which stayed at the top of the UK chartsfor three weeks that summer.

Our musician, pianist, accordionist and the concert party lefty intellectual was played by John Clegg, the butt of many of Windsor's "Mr La-di-da Gunner Graham" jibes. Dacca-born Dino Shafeek made the transition from Indian student in LWT's *Mind Your Language* to the BBC to play the concert party char wallah. Barbar Bhatti, originally from Pakistan, had qualified as an architect and, with his brother, was running an Indian restaurant in the Kings Road when David and Jimmy promoted him to the officer's punkah wallah Rumzan.

From this mixture of ages, nationalities, backgrounds, experience and training, Croft and Perry conjured the opening show over Christmas and New Year in 1972-73. I returned to *A Flea In Her Ear* in Leeds, and waited. Would it, would it not be a series?

They took months, but eventually clearance came through from the executives on the top floor of the TV Centre for an initial series of eight episodes. It was one of the happiest shows I've ever had the good fortune to work on. My fellow squaddies made sure no one ever got above himself, and Windsor, Michael and our captain and colonel showed us all how to play television comedy. We made fifty-six episodes over the next nine years.

London, 1974-81.

THE DAY WINDSOR DAVIES GOT ME ARRESTED

The crowded courtroom was quieted by the chief usher. The dignified gentleman on the bench, acutely aware of the silence and tension in the room, focused over the rim of his glasses to the shame-faced occupant of the dock. Satisfied that the silenced courtroom was now showing sufficient respect to the law of the land and its vital work, he paused, then lifted his head and announced the verdict.

"Drunk in Leicester Square. Fined two pounds. Next!"

My shame was complete. And it was all Windsor Davies's fault.

A casting director called Allan Foenander nursed a dream of having as many of the cast of *It Ain't Half Hot, Mum* in the same TV ad at the same time. So, from time to time, some of the lads, usually Chris Mitchell, who played Parky, the sergeant major's possible illegitimate son, Ken MacDonald who played Nobby, and myself were summoned to Soho for an advert audition. On this occasion, the advert, for Guinness, required a loud, bullying authoritative figure, so naturally the sergeant major, Windsor Davies, was invited along as well.

There is a special talent to auditioning for adverts.

Chris and Windsor were very good at it. I was not. But the master, the main man, the undisputed king of the advert audition was Ken MacDonald. I watched in awe as Ken, in a matter of seconds, had the committee of advertising agency talent, the casting director and the clients convinced that only he could do justice to this gem of a script, this unique and original concept, this potentially award-winning sixty-second slice of genius.

During the eight-year run of IAHHM, Ken popped up in dozens of TV and cinema ads, on commercial radio, in newspapers and magazines. You would bump into life-size cardboard Ken MacDonalds in shops and stores, part of displays urging you to invest in TV rentals, or soup or soap. I was certainly jealous of his success, but had to acknowledge he was a master of that particular art.

After he worked his magic on the Guinness people, we all filed out into the mid-afternoon Soho air. What to do now? "I know of a club," volunteered our sergeant major.

Fatal.

I know it seems out of the dark ages, but there was a time when licensing hours dictated that you could only drink in pubs at certain times of the day, usually eleven in the morning to three in the afternoon, and five until eleven in the evening. So drinking "clubs" were created to get round the law. If you were a bona fide club member paying a subscription, you and the friends you signed in could drink round the clock. Windsor knew of one such place. Off we went. I had heard of this club. It had a large membership, mostly actors, who spent many hours in its gloomy and malodorous environs. One very famous actor, introduced to the place by a colleague, is reputed to have asked: "What IS that very odd smell?"

"Failure," came the reply.

Windsor's capacity for beer was phenomenal. Maybe it was simply to do with him being London Welsh, but he could drink pint after pint in quantities that would have anyone else hospitalised. He was also terrific company, which helped. So, hours later, after Chris and Ken had wandered woozily into the night, and Windsor had set off to Victoria station and home, I was still sitting at our table, trying to make up my mind where I was and how I had got there.

I had a choice, I decided: go home to my wife and flat in Brentford, or try the Opera Tavern in Drury Lane to meet other mates for one last drink. I hit the night air and everything somehow became more difficult, making decisions and walking, to name but two. I had changed my mind and direction at least four times before I dropped my cigarettes. I reckon that's what drew the policeman's attention. I smoked French Disque Bleu cigarettes at that time – and that wasn't the only pretentious thing about me – and they had a habit of slipping out of their soft-top packet if you didn't keep an eye on them.

So there I was, doing a reasonable impersonation of some disorientated long-legged wading bird, trying to retrieve the French fags that had fallen from my inebriated grasp, when I heard a strong Scottish voice ask: "You. What's yer name and address?" He was a very young lad. Big, though, and sturdily built. But I knew my rights. I hadn't broken any law, and my name and address were my own private business.

"'Snone of your business," I enunciated carefully.

He repeated: "What's yer name and address?"

"Why?"

"Because if you don't give me yer name and address, Ah'm gonna arrest ye fur being drunk."

I had him there. I knew he definitely couldn't do that. You had to be doing something anti-social, usually related to careless bladder control while inebriated, before he could arrest you.

"You can't do that," I said. "You can't arrest me for just being dr... Ooyah!"

He was very quick. He had my arm up my back and had hoisted me in a tightish half-nelson and was off down the street with me before I could react. I held on to the Disque Bleu packet, though.

We were heading through Covent Garden in no time at all. I glanced back at the determined Scottish face, now a little flushed by the effort involved. I, on the other hand, was expending no energy at all. My toes were barely touching the pavement, thanks to the half-nelson.

An American tourist came up to him, saying: "Excuse me, officer..."

"Sorry," said my Scottish captor. "I have a prisoner!"

A prisoner? Moi? Oh please...

His destination, quickly reached, was Bow Street nick. I was introduced to the desk sergeant, who didn't seem too pleased with the extra paperwork his young colleague had lumbered him with. Closer inspection of the arresting officer's hat showed tell-tale traces of the light blue thread that had until quite recently kept his probationary hat-band in place. I had sobered up a bit during the enforced arm-up-the-back stroll from Soho and was more than happy now to give the desk sergeant my full name and address. The trouble that was going to get me into... I was still convinced, however, that I could not be arrested for just being drunk, so sat in my cell complaining to myself for hours. Meanwhile, the Brentford police had been told who I was and where I lived, and one of their number was sent along to tell my wife Annie where I was, out so late on a Thursday night. Unfortunately, they couldn't or wouldn't tell her why I had been nicked, or what kind of condition I was in. Panicking, she enlisted the help of a kindly neighbour, John Dann, who drove her to Bow Street, where the desk sergeant was only too happy to tell her. Drunk.

She was absolutely fizzing. On our way home, I was amazed no one would speak to me, considering the gross injustice to which I had been subjected by these fascist bastards… etc, etc. I was in full argumentative flow in the back of John's car when Annie, her face flushed with rage, turned round from the front seat and screamed: "SHUT UP, STUART, JUST FUCKING SHUT UP!!"

It was the angriest I had ever seen her. I kept very quiet for the rest of the journey home.

Kindly neighbour John had persuaded the desk sergeant to postpone my upcoming court appearance for twenty-four hours because I was due in studio the next day for the weekly recording of IAHHM at the Television Centre, Wood Lane. Next morning, studio day, I was not at my best. Horribly hungover, suffering from a blinding headache, delicate stomach, and a persistent pain in my half-nelson arm, there were other things I should have been doing, like just sleeping.

To make matters a million times worse, that week's episode – "Front Line Entertainers", episode one, series five – involved a rail trip up country, shot on a three-sided mock-up of an Indian railway carriage. To create the rocking rhythm of an Indian train trip, the whole thing was on springs. To make the carriage bounce about, out of shot the stage hands jumped up and down on it. It was the longest studio day of all the episodes of all the series. Comedy? I had to get off that train so many times, queasily squeezing past Windsor and Ken and Chris, happily none of them any the worse for their afternoon in Soho.

Next day, Saturday morning, I'd had a sober twenty-four hours to consider the folly of my actions before joining the morning parade of shamefaced drunks, pissers up alleyways, breachers of the peace, and hung-over celebrants in front of the beak – a magistrate in this case. No evidence offered, a plea of guilty accepted.

"Fined two pounds. Next!"

I had a criminal record, all the fault of that Windsor Davies. "I know a place", indeed. And yes, you can be arrested for just being drunk. I have the record to prove it.

London, 1975.

THE POTATO HOLIDAYS

Sounds positively feudal now, but when I was a youngster, all the schools in our part of Scotland were closed for two weeks at the end of October. The reason? To allow us all out to help gather in the most important crop of the farming year – potatoes. Mums, Dads, school kids, pensioners, weans, babies in buggies, everyone was called on for two weeks – sometimes three if the weather was really bad – for the annual tattie holidays.

In my village, two farms competed for the labour, Crosston and Drummie. It was a rural Old Firm competitiveness: any time the workers' tractors and carts from the rival farms met in the village, spuds and other missiles were exchanged. The crop was vital to the area. Not only were the farmers' bank balances held hostage by the tatties, but almost every household in the village depended on this annual two weeks of income. Winter coats and boots for the kids, housekeeping necessities, and Christmas presents for the family.

In the absence of any health and safety regulations, the tatties were exciting. The tractors and carts would pick up the tattie pickers, or "howkers", from agreed collection points around the village. It was early, still not full daylight, damp and cold. If it was raining, you sometimes, only sometimes, had the luxury of a tarpaulin cover on the cart for shelter. Each howker had a bag with food and drink for the rest of the day. Great chunky sandwiches, various fillings, maybe crisps and always sweeties. Plus, the vital vacuum flask full of something wet and hot. These flasks were notoriously fragile, not comfortable with rough treatment, and prone to shattering on the slightest contact. The worst thing you could do was bump your Thermos against something solid when climbing into the cart. The muffled noise – like tissue paper being squeezed – told you the glass inner of the flask was broken, and you faced a day without anything hot to drink. That was one long, thirsty day.

The cart didn't take long to fill up, helped by the odd buggie or pram with a baby in it, swaddled like an Eskimo child against the cold. Once at the field, the science of the delegation of work was not complex. The foreman, or gaffer or grieve, counted the number of pickers, and divided the length of the field by that number into "bits". Each adult had a whole bit, each child a half bit. Families were kept together. Troublemakers kept apart. Our foreman, Mr Fenton, would collect an armful of whins, and each whin, or pinny, stuck in the ground, marked the start of your bit, and the end of your neighbour's.

The bits settled, enter the digger. The cold, remorseless digger, usually driven by a mad person.

Before progress intervened, the digger was appropriately called "The Scatterer". Towed the length of the drill behind the tractor, it was simply a rimless wheel, whose revolving spokes hurled the potatoes, stones, and dirt out at right angles. The scatterer was driveshaft driven, which meant the faster the tractor went, the further the potatoes were hurled. The picker's job was to retrieve the potatoes and put them in a wicker basket called a skull. This, he or she had to do as quickly as possible, as the digger was followed by another tractor, towing a cart, attended by a couple of muscly lads whose job was to empty the skulls into the cart.

Almost immediately, along came the digger again.

Sounds idyllic, put like that. A bucolic scene of innocent sunlit rustic labour worthy of a Gainsborough or a Turner.

You could try this at home: stretch your legs out at either side and lean forward until your hands are touching the floor beneath you. Then stretch alternately to either side and as far forward as you can reach, returning after each stretch to the central, bent-over position. Do this for four or five metres, at the same time heaving an increasingly heavy laundry basket in front of you. For perfect verisimilitude, do this out in the open on a dull, cold, drizzly day.

For eight hours.

The weather was key. Scotland in late autumn gives you all sorts of weather each day, and it usually involves rainfall. The misery of a day spent in damp clothes in a constant, gusting wind, with mud all round, on boots and knees and fingers and eyes – and your Thermos out of action – deserves a description by Dickens. However, on a sunny day high on a warm hillside on the east coast of Scotland, with the smell of the good earth and an arrowhead skein of geese overhead flying south for the winter, and your Thermos unbroken and that bit of chocolate not yet started, and your wages at the end of the week, it was good to be alive.

There were other distractions for a kid at the tatties.

The adults' language was always interesting. The ability of many a Scotsman, especially land-reared hard-working hard-drinking Scotsmen, to string together a coherent conversation almost exclusively consisting of cuss words is legendary. It wasn't that we children had never heard these words, in isolation, before, but this strung-together avalanche, this torrent of blasphemy and obscenity was a revelation. And, we discovered quickly, a revelation not to be tried at home.

And there was always the "shove a mouse down your knickers" game. This involved one of the muscly skull-chuckers pretending he had a mouse in his hands, which he was going to shove down the knickers of a yet-unchosen victim. All knicker-wearers, regardless of age or marital status, were considered potential targets. The game involved a lot of chasing and a great deal of very loud, hysterical screaming. In spite of the rough ground, the ladies usually avoided capture by displaying a remarkable turn of speed and agility, considering their weight and girth, and in spite of the extra handicap of heavy overcoats and wellingtons.

Other diversions included fires, started by burning the withered shaws of the potatoes and anything else flammable. A good-going fire would roast potatoes, eventually, and the choking smoke from a slow-burning fire would provide entertainment for the kiddies by annoying the adults. Sabotage often slowed down production. A well-placed boulder, buried and camouflaged in the drill, and unseen by the ever-alert mad digger driver, could break or bend a spoke on the Scatterer, and require on-field repairs.

In later years, the Scatterer was replaced by the more sophisticated Elevator digger, which scooped up earth, stones, shaws, and potatoes on to a conveyor belt of metal links. The earth fell between the links, leaving a neat drill's-width of potatoes, all within easy reach of the picker. Much more efficient, and much less painful on the leg muscles. And the Elevator, with its many linked moving parts, was more vulnerable to the juvenile, booby-trapping saboteurs. Smaller rocks were easier to come by, harder to extract, and equally efficient.

The day's labour was broken by an hour for lunch, and a mid-morning and mid-afternoon break: "Piecey time". Bartering took place – your cheese sandwich for my KitKat. Your half-tube of Spangles for my half-roasted potato from the fire. Food never tasted so good.

At the end of the day, each lady picker was allowed a "boiling" of potatoes to take home for the family. This freebie was policed by the gaffer, and rarely exploited, but now and then a buggy or pram would wobble homeward, suspiciously low on its straining springs. The odd howker, too, would leave the field with a piecey-bag a lot heavier than when he arrived.

Last year, I watched the potato harvest on the same fields. No howkers, no children, no mothers, no muscly skull-chuckers, no screams, no fires, no babies in prams or buggies. Just a machine driving up and down the field, harvesting the potatoes directly into wooden pallets towed by another tractor, to be directed to the nearest temperature-controlled store. Two machines, two drivers, one contractor. Soulless.

One of the saddest things I've ever seen…

DEATH BY BLOOD CAPSULE

My drama school was a College when I was there. After I left, it promoted itself to Academy, and then, wait for it, a Conservatoire.

We were cast in a production of a weird French piece, which I didn't understand then and still don't, called Chez Torpe, by Francois Billetdoux. It involved a policeman's investigation of a hotel where, it seems, people come to commit suicide. The inspector turns up in act one to investigate one death, and by the end of act three, another of the guests – we'll call him Hans – shoots himself. Hans was played by a young man – let's call him Charlie – who took it all very seriously and who went to great lengths to be utterly convincing. Unfortunately, he was also devoid of any vestige of common sense, which made him potentially dangerous not only to himself, but also to the rest of us.

The plot demands that the actor playing Hans shoot himself in the head on the darkened half-landing leading from the hotel lounge to the bedrooms. Charlie, in the first of many miscalculations, thought it would be even more compelling if, having shot himself, he would tumble down the stairs, fatally wounded. And yes, of course, he would be bleeding. The rest of the cast advised against it, suggesting that blowing his brains out on the darkened half-landing and leaving it at that would allow the rest of us to get on with the play. Our director was all for artists expressing themselves, so...

Like all good detective story denouements, the entire cast is on stage to hear the inspector's conclusions. Under cover of the interminable French dialogue, Charlie – Hans – makes his way unobserved to the half-landing. So far, so good. Then, for a page before the shooting, we are all upstaged by the clearly audible rustling of cellophane coming from Hans, bent over suspiciously in the dark. The inspector raises his voice to cover this unwanted noise, but by now the audience has picked up on it too. This isn't in the script. Then we discover it's only Charlie, true to form, wrestling with the crinkly plastic wrapping round his blood capsule.

Our inspector ploughs on with his findings. There's an increase of tension on stage because we all know the gunshot is coming up. Charlie must have popped the effervescent blood capsule into his mouth and bitten on it by now, and he should be clasping the starting pistol we were using to mimic the revolver. Now, we've all seen starting pistols used at athletics meetings. There's a reason the starter points the pistol up in the air, as far away from himself as possible. Bits of cartridge paper are blown out of the gun by the blast. However, in the interests of verisimilitude, and faithfulness to the drama, Charlie chose to point the gun close to his head. There was a very realistic bang, followed by exclamations of "Ooyah! Ooyah!" and the sound of Charlie slapping and rubbing his perforated scalp.

He quickly realised that "Ooyah" might not be an accurate response to blowing your brains out, and so, disorientated and slightly panicked, he set off on his dramatic collapse down the stairs. There were only about half a dozen steps, but Charlie managed to hit every one of them, quite hard, on the way down. Had he not alienated the entire cast by this point, there might have been more sympathy for him, but we watched with an almost detached disregard as Charlie eventually came to rest at the foot of the stairs, head down, feet up, and facing the audience. A very convincing fall and a believable corpse.

In the action of the play, there is, of course, a horrified pause as the hotel guests take on board the tragedy they have just witnessed. Before anyone could speak, however, we watched as the corpse's effervescent blood capsule, now in full fizziness, leaked out of his upside-down mouth and dribbled, unhindered, into his nose. We watched, grimly fascinated, like a snake transfixed in front of a mongoose, as Charlie's nose began blowing big crimson blood bubbles. Charlie, with the entire cast and audience looking on, was drowning.

Although it was tempting to leave him there, bubbling and suffering with his brains blown out, we had to get on with the now seriously derailed play, so our inspector, in a moment of compassion for a fellow actor, turned Charlie over with his foot. The corpse's chest heaved with gratitude as he now lay face-down, gulping in huge lungfuls of air. The cast regrouped and lurched towards the end of the play. Charlie, now fully recovered, joined us all for the curtain call, bobbing up and down, bloodied and bowing, supremely confident of his contribution to the evening's success, and completely unaware that the performance he had just given had very nearly been his last.

Glasgow, 1965.

PERCY EDWARDS, MBE

One of the great joys of *Play School* during my eight years of co-presenting was the range of visiting artists who came in to demonstrate their various skills, or tell a story to camera. These stories were sometimes a complete nightmare. We rehearsed all five weekly programmes in one day in the Fun Factory in North Acton on the Friday. The weekend was spent trying to learn them, and on Monday we recorded the first two, on Tuesday two more, and the final one on Wednesday.

Any relief from this performing treadmill was always welcomed, and a story entrusted to a visiting guest was one fewer for us to learn.

Perhaps difficult to believe now, but we were never allowed the luxury of autocue. The autocue machine came complete with a costly autocue machine operator and the *Play School* budget couldn't run to that kind of expense. A story to camera was precisely that. There was just you, full-face, and one camera, no cutaways or useful editing points. Just you and the camera, and there could be an awful lot of story. Any slip, stumble, hesitation or just forgetting what comes next, and you had to go all the way back to the beginning. A story to camera could be a real nerve-shredder.

Percy Edwards made his name on radio and in the

variety theatre by being able to mimic the calls of up to 600 birds and countless animals, and for our purposes he could mimic the soundscape of domestic appliances. He was also a respected ornithologist and a fellow of the Zoological Society of London. The story Percy was asked to tell involved bird and animal sounds, plus appliances. The director of this particular week was a Welsh lady renowned for her robust approach to her performers.

Percy was a gentle, mild-mannered East Anglian, and at the rehearsals we watched with some interest as the personalities confronted each other. The first move the director made was strong. She turned a chair round, and sat astride it, the chair's back and her front facing Percy. I could tell Percy was puzzled by this unnecessary pressure. They worked their way through the story.

"Then," said the powerfully positioned director, "the girl helps her mother do the laundry by switching on the washing machine. You know, Percy, ka-dugadugadugadug."

I couldn't believe it. She was imitating a washing machine, telling Percy how to do his job. He was equal to it, though.

"No, my dear," he said gently. "That's not entirely accurate. I think you'll find that's a tumble dryer."

In a break from rehearsals, I chatted to Percy in the studio coffee bar about living in East Anglia. I had recently bought a place there, mainly thanks to the BBC.

The BBC Wood Lane Television Centre, alas, no longer with us, was a wondrous place to a young actor. Circular in shape, the ground floor housed eight studios of differing sizes, some big enough for the most elaborate extravaganzas, others small enough for shows such as *Play School*. Round the outside ran the notorious ring road, for moving complete sets, props and banks of seats in and out of the studios. Any time a director complained about the non-arrival of an essential prop or set, the excuse was always: "It's on the ring road."

Dressing rooms and wardrobe and make-up departments were one floor down in the basement, and outside every studio there was a handy coffee bar, where I mentioned to Percy that the peace of our East Anglian village, Worlingworth, was being routinely disturbed by a local peacock, looking for a mate. The queue for the tea bar inched forward.

"Oh yes," said Percy, "the peacock at rut is a very noisy bird."

With that, without warning, he threw his head back and uttered, at extraordinary volume, the anguished cry of the love-lorn peacock.

"HOLY MARY, MOTHER OF GOD," screamed a large black lady behind him, at the same time letting go of a huge tray of cutlery, crockery and glasses destined for the dishwasher. The crash was enormous and went on for ages as the queue jumped out of the way and into each other, crunching over the debris. Percy was appalled and contrite as he helped the tea bar assistant recover.

"My dear, I'm so sorry. So sorry. I had no idea..."

"Was that you?" she said. "Did you make that noise?"

"Well, yes," said Percy lamely. "It's... it's what I do."

When not bringing uppity directors gently down to size, or scaring tea ladies, Percy had a fund of ornithological stories. One involved a talk he gave to a branch of the Royal Society for the Protection of Birds, complete with impersonations. The lady in charge was very anxious that her star guest visit her house to see the lengths to which she had gone to attract and feed the local wildlife, especially the birds. Percy, polite as ever, explained to her that he would love to, but they had run out of time if he was to catch his train home. Disappointed but obliging, his hostess drove him to the station. As he presented his ticket to the collector at the barrier, she persevered.

"Next time you come to see us, Mr Edwards," she gushed, "you simply must come to my house to see my tits."

The ticket collector, reported Percy, was struck dumb.

London, 1979.

THE CRICH TRAM MUSEUM

Early in 1983, I was asked to be in *Grey Granite* by BBC Scotland. It was a television adaptation of *A Scots Quair,* by Lewis Grassic Gibbon. *Grey Granite* was the third book of the trilogy. The first book, *Sunset Song,* had been made some ten years earlier to great acclaim. The second, *Cloud Howe,* had been equally successful, and BBC Scotland decided to cash in while the going was good to make the third.

I had given Tom Cotter, the director of books two and three, a very hard time while casting *Cloud Howe*. At drama college, I had been told by one instructor that I had "an emotional quality of the suffering type", and in *Cloud Howe* there was a part fit, as they say, to tear a cat in. A youngish Church of Scotland minister, the Rev Robert Colquhoun, suffered a major crisis of conscience and faith in the aftermath of the First World War. Right up my street, I thought modestly, and pursued Mr Cotter for all I was worth to let me play Colquhoun. Nowadays, I suppose it would be called stalking. I failed. He gave the part to Hugh Fraser, who rewarded his director by turning in a beautiful. performance.

However, in book three, *Grey Granite,* there was the equally good, if not better, part of Jim Trease, the local Communist Party organiser and agitator. Given my known abrasive campaigning style and serious nuisance qualities, Tom asked me to play him.

The shoot, mainly in Aberdeen, which is entirely made of grey granite, was a blast. The original books are a joy to read, lyrical, hard-headed and witty in equal measure, and our adaptor, Bill Craig, had encapsulated all of these tricky qualities in his script. Our last day of filming had to be in Derbyshire, because that's where the trams were.

Our story required a Communist-inspired protest demonstration against the means-testing of soldiers' benefits after the First World War, and our director and location managers had come up with a couple of genuine retired Glasgow trams in the tram museum at Crich,

It was a tough morning. Extras, or non-speaking artistes as they are known nowadays, arrived by the busload to be dressed, made up and then directed. They quickly had to learn *The Internationale,* to be sung, raggedly, on the hoof, while avoiding moving trams and police escorts.

I thought they were terrific, the extras, and told them so at the lunch break. They were suitably modest, and then mentioned that some of their very best work could soon be seen in several episodes of *Tinker Tailor Soldier Spy,* set, supposedly, in East Berlin, Highly recommended, they said.

Chatting and smoking after lunch, the non-speaking artistes were intrigued to observe several horseboxes arrive and unload their cargo. Some of them even recognised that doyen of stuntmen, Nosher Powell, with some half-dozen equally muscular colleagues, all in full police gear. I had seen the full script and read the original book. The extras, I suspected, had not. "They'll be here for the mounted policemen baton charge," I told them.

"Eh?"

"The baton charge," I said. "When the mounted police charge the demonstration."

Remarkably, no one batted an eyelid. These were real pros. If the script called for a baton charge, so be it.

The afternoon was furiously busy. *The Internationale* was sung again and again. Police sergeant Nosher Powell halted the demonstrators and read the Riot Act, calling on them to disperse, or else. The demonstrators stood firm, resolute, encouraged by that unscrupulous Commie, Jim Trease.

It's not something you can fake, a horseback baton charge. I mean, there has to be contact, and there was: lots of it. The extras were magnificent, grabbing on to the bridles, trying to dislodge the coppers. Organised bedlam. After one particularly energetic take, an appalled Jim Trease swung into agitator mode. I was pretty certain that if the BBC thought it could get away with paying the extras only the basic minimum, it would.

"This isn't just extra-ing," I said. "This is more like stunt work. Are you sure you're getting the proper rate for the job?"

"Oh, I think we'll get the right money," said my friend from the lunch break. "The boss of our agency is here with us."

"Great," I said, looking at the crowd of spectators. "Where is he?"

"Over there, flat on his back on the ground," he replied. "Being treated by the St John people. Whatever the best rate for today's work is, I think we're going to get it. Don't you?"

Derbyshire, 1983.

Postscript:

The director of *Sunset Song*, the first book in the trilogy, was the then-head of drama at BBC Scotland, the redoubtable Pharic Maclaren. Pharic directed from a wheelchair, a victim of the poliomyelitis epidemic in his childhood, which killed and damaged hundreds. Because the employment of so many actors was in his gift, and thanks to the wickedness and dark humour of Glasgow, his popular nickname was "Meals on Wheels".

THE RSC HITS DETROIT

Seven weeks in Los Angeles in January and February, one paltry week in beautiful San Francisco, and then Detroit, Michigan, for six weeks, to be followed by three weeks in New Haven. No one was thrilled about Detroit in March. After the comparative warmth of the West Coast, Detroit was bitterly cold, with the wind whistling off Lake St Clair. Many of the cast, including me, had enthusiastically embraced the West Coast hippy lifestyle. I'd fallen for long hair, kaftans and beads and love and peace, man. I had danced in Los Angeles on the stage of Hair with co-author Gerome Ragni, for goodness sake!

All we had to look forward to in Detroit was the commemoration on April 4 of Martin Luther King's murder the previous year. On arrival, we were told to stay indoors and keep warm, and instructed to ignore the gunshots outside. All the married men with wives and families on the tour sent them home from San Francisco. The single guys, too, had said goodbye to girlfriends found in either Los Angeles or San Francisco or, in some cases, both. The fun part of the tour, we feared, was over.

Even being billeted in one of the city's finest hotels, the Leland on 400 Bagley Street, could not raise our spirits. We were booked to spend over a month here, with two plays we'd premiered the previous year, were advised not to go out much, and on top of that, were deprived of the comfort of wives and girlfriends. Slowly and morosely, having checked in and dumped our luggage, the guys in the company filtered down to the coffee shop on the ground floor, and sat in L-shaped Edward Hopper silent misery, deep in our collective gloom. Meanwhile, unbidden, unexpected and initially unnoticed by the self-pitying thespians, outside the main entrance of the hotel, two massive luxury coaches pulled up and disgorged their passengers. I could not believe my eyes. I nudged my neighbour for confirmation to make sure I wasn't dreaming. "Can you see what I see?"

He blinked to double-check. Yes, he could. The most glamorous, exotic and beautiful girls, and boys, most of them in full show-time make-up, stepped out of the coaches and on to the sidewalk and into our hotel. Behind them, the coaches bore the legend: "THE FABULOUS ICE CAPADES!"

The Ice Capades was a long-established touring iceskating company, led by former Olympic and world champions, presenting shows of spectacular skating skills, athleticism, comedy and glamour. Especially glamour. The girls were contractually obliged to wear full show-time make-up whenever seen in public. And they were booked in to the Leland on Bagley for almost the full length of our stay.

There was someone for everyone.

After a silent prayer of thanks to the God of our understanding, we introduced ourselves, and over the next few days, discovered that the Ice Capades were bored with touring and also anxious to know more Shakespeare, one way or another. The companies integrated along casting lines. The leading actors squired the leading dancers, and so on down the cast list. This meant that the spear carriers got to know the chorus girls, and I don't recall anyone complaining. And they all had such wonderful dancers' legs. Now, I come from the east coast of Scotland, and the nature of the work available to girls over the generations – shops, farming, nursing, even teaching – means long hours on your feet. The result? Fluid. No knees and no ankles. The legs go straight down from hip to shoe. Smooth curves and dimples and indentations are unheard of.

But the Ice Capades, man, they were all leg. Muscular, toned, shapely and beautiful athletes atop muscular, toned, shapely and beautiful legs. And they were booked into the Leland Bagley!

My Ice Capade was called Sue-Anne. A tall, blonde girl, originally from Texas, she bore more than a passing resemblance to Marilyn Monroe. Her best friend, who quickly became my best friend Glynn's very best friend, was a smaller, feisty, dark-haired girl from the Bronx called Ruth. When they weren't rehearsing – they worked incredibly hard – and we weren't called for understudy rehearsals, which wasn't often, we compared our various skills. The girls learned about iambic pentameter and stage fighting, while Glynn and I became familiar with the double salchow and the triple loop. Not for the first time on this tour, I would find myself smugly glancing to the heavens and thinking: "No' bad for a wee boy from Letham!"

While in San Francisco, I had become very close to an actress with the American Conservatory Theatre

Company, headed by Bill Ball on Geary Street, whom I shall call Hilary. We parted sadly at the end of our brief visit, promising to keep in touch. Midway through the Detroit part of the tour, Hilary phoned to say she'd be flying in to the Leland Bagley early the following morning. And she had a really "cool" present with her. Panic. I had promised to be with Sue-Anne. I had not mentioned any previous girlfriend on any other part of the tour. What to do?

I was amazed at the mobility and independence of your average American girl. When touring in Britain, you could have an affair in Birmingham and never expect the girl to turn up, virtually unannounced, in, say, Glasgow. But in the US? A flight from San Francisco to Detroit is over two thousand miles. And Hilary was on it!

I considered my options, all of which involved lying. On the other hand, I was a recently born-again hippy. Ever since seeing Hair in Los Angeles, I'd happily adopted the whole "Peace, Truth and Love" philosophy. Here was a chance to put it into action. I explained to Sue-Anne who Hilary was and that she was arriving in a few short hours.

To my utter amazement, Sue-Anne said it wasn't a problem. Not only was it not a problem, she suggested I make it look as if my bed was being slept in by me, and I should stay with her, Sue-Anne, until Hilary arrived in the early hours of the morning, at which point I could go down to the lobby and greet her. She, Sue-Anne, would have calls to my room transferred to her room to facilitate this. I was gobsmacked. Amazing. Maybe there was something to this "Peace, Truth and Love" thing after all. So, for the next couple of days, Sue-Anne stayed quietly in the background, while Hilary, my friend Glynn and his friend Ruth and I enjoyed all the facilities of the hotel.

Late one evening, after a very lengthy visit to one of the hotel bars, Hilary remembered her present. Two tabsules of THC. I was quite underwhelmed, as alcohol was my drug of choice, even after Hilary excitedly explained that THC – tetrahydrocannabinol – is the active part of cannabis, and we were guaranteed a fine old time.

"But there are four of us."

"No problem," said Hilary. "I'll split the tabsules and we can snort them."

She duly made four little piles of the powder on different parts of the glass-topped table in my apartment and then asked if anyone had a crisp, fresh, dollar bill. Glynn produced a brand new one-hundred-dollar bill, and on Hilary's instruction, rolled it up into a tube and shoved one end of it up his nose. "Sniff it up!" yelled Hilary. Glynn duly did, followed by Ruth and then Hilary herself.

"Your turn," said Hilary to me. "Let's go!" I leaned towards the last pile of THC.

"Is all the air out of your lungs?" asked a now slightly manic Hilary.

"Yes!" I replied, blowing the pile all over the table-top.

"Goddam," shrieked Hillary, and brought the wayward powder back to the central sniff point. "Let's go! "

Now, the end of this one-hundred-dollar bill was no longer crisp. It had already been up three nostrils and was looking unappetisingly soggy and the worse for wear. The powder, too, had been all over the tabletop and as I leant forward, steeling myself to the cold clamminess of the bill going up my nose, I could see little glistening curls of hotel fluff sticking out of the powder.

"Let's go!" commanded Hilary. I sniffed it up - and immediately sneezed it all back down again.

"Goddam!" yelled Hilary, as Glynn and Ruth collapsed hysterically on the floor.

"I need a drink," I said.

All this was faithfully reported back to the amazing Sue-Anne when Hilary departed. A fine old time indeed. Sadly, though, the Ice Capades moved on to their next city, and the Royal Shakespeare Company US tour drew to a premature end. For reasons that were never satisfactorily explained to me, and I suspect to any of the spear carriers, the end of the tour to New Haven was cancelled. We were going home. Except that I wasn't.

I had wangled a job with the American Conservatory Theatre and Bill Ball back in San Francisco, my favourite town, after Glasgow, in the world. Having penned a cheeky letter of resignation to Trevor Nunn, regretfully turning down his generous offer of the less-than-pivotal part of the rat-catcher in next season's *Bartholomew Fair,* I jetted back to the West Coast to play and rehearse as cast, and, Gawdelpus, teach. Peace and Love, man...

Detroit, 1969.

DEAR BRUTUS

The time? May 1960.

The place? Kirriemuir, Angus, Scotland.

The occasion? The centenary of the birth of Kirriemuir's most famous son, Sir JM Barrie,

playwright, novelist, reviewer, author of *Peter Pan*.

To commemorate the birth of Sir James Matthew Barrie, it was decided to mount a production of one of his most famous plays, *Dear Brutus*, in Kirriemuir Town Hall. The cast was to be headed by Mr Barry Sinclair and Miss Sarah Churchill, famous, among other things, for being the daughter of Sir Winston Churchill. By all accounts, the first night was a bit of a shambles, with Miss Churchill appearing to have difficulty remembering the lines, the moves, and even, on occasion, where she was. So what had been a limited celebration of a local author suddenly attracted the attention of the notoriously hard-nosed Scottish press pack, who quickly found out where Kirriemuir was and besieged the town.

Miss Churchill, meanwhile, on the afternoon after the night before, was spotted at the open upstairs window of the Ogilvy Arms hotel. The whole town knew Miss Churchill was billeted in the Ogilvy, and many of them were now outside hoping to spot their famous, if not notorious, guest. Joining them, hungry for scandal, were

THERE SHE GOES
EFTER ER LADS!
OGILVY ARMS
DEAR BRUTUS

the gentlemen of the press. Hotel staff and theatre personnel were seen trying to restrain her, but with the added strength of the not entirely sober, Churchill's daughter was fending them off with her free hand. The other was protecting a glass of something medicinal. She reached the open window.

"Peasants!" she declared, with a clarity sadly missing from her performance the night before. "You're all bloody peasants!" Usually, such a statement would be regarded as deeply insulting and worthy of an angry response, but the assembled citizens of Kirriemuir considered the accusation and agreed that, on balance, checking out the boots, the wellies, the ex-army jackets and tweed bonnets, Miss Churchill was probably right. Eventually, she was persuaded back into the upstairs room, and the window was slammed shut. This was when my two older brothers got into the act.

The eldest, Jim, thought it would be a great wheeze to drive into the car park behind the Ogilvy Arms hotel, where my second eldest brother, Bill, in the back of the car, would pull a tartan travel rug over his head. Jim would then accelerate out of the car park past the assembled throng at the front of the hotel. "There she goes," shouted the mob, and the press pack dashed to their cars. No one took the time to question whether Miss Sarah Churchill would even know what a Ford Anglia looked like, far less be agreeable to be driven across the Scottish countryside at speed in the back of one, but it was many miles later, almost as far as Forfar, before the reporters caught up with Jim and Bill. Expletives were exchanged.

I would love to report that Miss Churchill's minders took advantage of the decoy car with Bill in the back and spirited her out of Kirriemuir, but she left, quietly but publicly, the next day. Her place in *Dear Brutus* at the town hall was taken at ridiculously short notice by an actress from the nearby Pitlochry Festival Theatre, and Mr Barry Sinclair returned often to Kirriemuir in subsequent years to direct the annual offerings of the Kirriemuir Amateur Operatic Society.

Kirriemuir, 1960.

THE RSC HITS LA!

he green room in Stratford-upon-Avon was legendary. It was run by a benevolent dictator called Gladys, who looked after her staff and customers – actors, stagehands, electricians, sound engineers, musicians, stage management, wardrobe – without fear or favour. Food and alcohol and other refreshments were served throughout the performances, and it was a brave customer who ever got out of line with Gladys. So when the Royal Shakespeare Company arrived in Los Angeles at the Dorothy Chandler Pavilion and discovered there was NO green room, we were distraught. Instead of Gladys telling you you'd had enough, there was a soul-less corridor and a row of vending machines, dispensing all manner of cellophane-wrapped goodies. And no alcohol.

The star attraction, and remember this was 1969, was a state-of-the-art Coca-Cola dispenser. It was a marvel of construction and New World efficiency. Insert a coin, and it whirred and clunked into life. First came the plastic beaker, dropping snugly into its berth behind the little window. A moment later, from another source, came the crushed ice, followed swiftly by a precise measure of the syrupy base. Another tap then dispensed the clear lemonadey soda. The cup filled exactly to the brim, with just enough slight bubbly overflow to match all the Coke advertisements. Genius.

Bernie Lloyd, the effervescent Welshman who brilliantly played Claudio, was ahead of me in the queue. In went the coin, down came the crushed ice, out came the syrup and the final *pièce de resistance,* the precise measure of soda. The only thing that didn't come out was the cup. Bernie watched with increasing incredulity as ice, syrup and soda poured out of the taps and vanished down the plug hole behind the window. Then he turned to me and said, in his lilting Welsh accent: "Automation. Bloody marvellous, isn't it? Not only pours it for you, bloody drinks it for you as well!"

Halfway through the run, when *Faustus* and *Much Ado* alternated in performance, there was added drama when we managed, on stage, to accidentally set fire to a monk. There's a deeply irreverent scene in *Faustus* where Faust, played by Eric Porter, tells Mephistopheles, played by Terence Hardiman, that he wants to cause chaos in the Vatican. His wish is granted. Mephistopheles makes him invisible and Faust steals His Holiness's food, spills his drink, and "hits him a box of the ear". The pope retaliates by sending in a team of dirge-singing friars, to exorcise this demon.

Among the friars was a fellow spear carrier, Richard Jones Barry, and he was the one who burst into flames.

We worked out later what must have happened. As we all dashed on stage to purge the Vatican, Richard must have picked up a hastily discarded cigarette end in the hem of his cassock. (The Americans were extraordinarily security and fire-conscious. There were bins everywhere, and smoking was frowned upon in the building. We all smoked. This was 1969.) Back on stage, with Faustus causing mayhem at the pope's court, we monks went dashing from one devilish trick to another, from one side of the stage to the other, unwittingly fanning the smouldering embers in Jones Barry's cassock. There must have been a lot of wool in the fabric of the monk's garments, because the stage soon began to fill with the smell of burning sheep. The Californian audience, reverently following this classic company performing this classic play, stirred uneasily. Surely, if this was the Vatican, the air should be heavy with the smell of incense, not whatever this stuff was?

One final dash across stage, when Faustus delivered his "box of the ears," to the pope, and ignition point was reached. There was Jones Barry, spinning round and round trying to identify the source of the smoke and flames, and the rest of the friars, dirge-singing now completely forgotten, stamping on him, trying to put him out. Eric Porter, Terence Hardiman and Eric Allan, playing the pope, were left isolated and bemused while downstage a swirling mass of stamping, arm-waving monks, shrouded in acrid-smelling smoke, eventually succeeded in extinguishing Mr Jones Barry, and hefted him, still smouldering, into the wings.

Thereafter, exceptionally severe cigarette-smoking security was imposed by the Dorothy Chandler Pavilion. They weren't going to have a bunch of Limeys burning the place down.

Los Angeles, 1969.

GETTING LIFTED

Now, I know you'll never need this. You are far too responsible and mature and law-abiding to find yourself in this kind of awkward position, but I am going to proffer the advice anyway. If you ever find yourself woozily driving along the Wellesley Road in west London late on a Friday night, and a police car pulls abruptly in front of you and the officer says "We've had a few tonight, haven't we, sir?", do not, having at last got the window to roll down, reply, shrilly and happily: "Certainly have!"The next few hours, your life is not your own.

"My colleague will drive your car, sir, if you would kindly get in the back of mine," said the officer. "Oh, and just keep smiling, he'll be all right if you keep smiling."

On the back seat sat the biggest, hairiest, meanest-looking Alsatian I had ever come across, and he was growling. This was no ordinary growl. This didn't come from his throat, but from somewhere deep and profound and unfathomable in the darkest recesses of his bowels. This was a great *basso profondo* growl, reverberating through his entire shaggy frame, and it was aimed at me.

"Just keep smiling at it," said the officer. "He's gentle as a kitten, really."

The evening had begun so well. A friend and team-mate from our Sunday morning football team – Los Astros del Sol, out of the Sun In Splendour pub in Notting Hill – had officially opened his upmarket kitchenware shop, and we were there to help him celebrate. A very good and not entirely sober time was had by all. Cleverly, I had worked out that it would be safer not to drive past the Chiswick police station to get home. I would be wiser to use the quieter, safer, Wellesley Road. And now here I was, clinging on to a frayed rictus of a smile and hoping the dog would not rip out my throat as we swung into the Chiswick police station car park.

The paperwork took no time at all, and then we had to await the arrival of a doctor. As well as being breathalysed, suspects had to give two samples of blood, one for the police to confirm the over-the-limit alcohol level, and one for the suspect to have independently analysed. I could tell the doctor, an elderly and distinguished man, by my guess originally from the Indian sub-continent, was not happy. I spotted pyjamas peeping out at the bottom of his trouser legs, a sure sign his sleep had been interrupted by this call-out. His job was just to take the blood for analysis. His judgment on the case in hand was not required, so there was some surprise from all of us when, as he left, he turned at the door and cried "He's pissed. Absolutely pissed", and stomped off, pyjamas still showing.

Two days later, a policeman came to my flat with details of the court case, which clashed with the upcoming filming of *It Ain't Half Hot, Mum*. "I'm contracted to be in Norfolk on that day to the BBC."

He refrained from saying "You should've thought of

that before you got pissed in Chiswick", but went on to explain that if I got a doctor's note saying I was too stressed to turn up on the allotted day but I'd be better a week later, I could postpone the hearing. "The real villains do it all the time," the policeman added. "No reason why you shouldn't get away with it."

Two weeks later, with the filming finished, I was banned for a year and fined. So remember. Anyone says "We've had a few tonight, sir", don't say…

Chiswick, 1972.

TALENTED HAIR

I've been lucky. I've always had very talented hair. Tony Smith, director of John Byrne's rock and roll saga *Tutti Frutti,* grabbed my hair at the audition and asked if would flatten when greased. I assured him it would. I got the part.

In the Sixties and Seventies, young men's hair was allowed to grow long. Footballer Kevin Keegan, among others, famously had his permed. Young actors, to be considered for contemporary parts (and also to improve their love life), had to have regulation trendy, flowing locks. Chances were, if you met a mate with short hair, he'd probably landed himself a part in some immediately pre or post-war drama. Eventually, the television companies had to add a clause to the actors' contracts, stating that by accepting the part and signing the contract, the artist agreed to have his hair cut to a length dictated by the director. This led to many an anguished debate among young actors. Should you accept a small part with short hair, thereby eliminating yourself from any contemporary parts until your hair had grown again?

The first contract-dictated short-hair job I had was in *Man of Straw,* the Thomas Mann novel set in Germany in the Thirties among the beer-drinking sabre-fighting student fraternity. It was produced by the BBC in 1972, with Derek Jacobi playing the lead, and directed by the inimitable Herbie Wise. Mr Wise, himself a fugitive from Nazi Germany, was a brilliant director. He had an unequalled gift of convincing you and everyone on the show that this was the best cast, this was the best crew, and the show, therefore, was going to be very, very special.

Come studio day and the suitably short-haired cast assembled for the first of many *Bierkeller* scenes. The students, under instruction from the "Fox-Major" – me – were required to quaff huge steins of lager inside a strict time limit, thereby proving both their manhood and their astonishing bladder control. Even higher male status was then achieved by going out and fighting each other with sabres and showing off the resultant scars. Mr Wise had somehow persuaded the BBC that genuine authenticity could only be achieved by using real German beer, so a dozen young short-haired actors were introduced to the pleasures of consuming draught Lowenbrau, common enough now but new to us all then. I think his argument was that it was easier to drink beer than water or some studio concoction in take after take. We all agreed, of course.

From what I can remember, the first studio day passed very quickly and happily. There was a reckoning the next morning, however. A couple of the actors had got into a fight on the Tube on the way home and were sporting several bruises and facial abrasions, covered now in very non-period and non-continuity Elastoplast. Another young man disappeared altogether, never to return. The rest of us were in a variety of hungover states and not relishing another encounter with the draught Lowenbrau. Only a combination of youthful resilience, a developing taste for Lowenbrau, and a crucial desire not to let down our greatly admired director saw us through to produce very effective scenes inside a very fine production.

Four years later, Messrs Wise and Jacobi combined to give us *I Claudius*.

While the hair on my head might have been talented, facial hair was a huge problem for me. I just couldn't grow it. My defence was always that I had better things to do with my hormones than shove hair out of my face. On the first days of rehearsals for *King Lear* for the RSC in 1968, all the men were told not to shave or have a haircut. This was going to be a hairy *King Lear*. A month later, we were all lined up in front of the make-up and wigs department. All my colleagues were, by this time, sporting fine beards and moustaches.

I was not looking forward to this. I got to the front of the line, the wig lady glanced up, frowned, and said: "I thought you were told not to shave." Sniggers all round. "I haven't shaved. If you look closely, you'll see. Look," I said, pointing to the downy upper lip. "If I turn my face to the light, can you see?" She sighed, and wrote in her beard and moustache book, and then said: "Next."

All that season, I had to wear false beards and moustaches, and it was a very hirsute season. For almost every show I braced myself for the application of spirit gum, which nipped like hell, to my cheeks, chin and upper lip. After the show, I braced myself again for the application of surgical spirit, which also nipped like hell, to remove the spirit gum. They were putting men on the moon, for God's sake! Could no one invent an adhesive that didn't hurt? After the curtain came down on the last *Lear*, I flushed my beard and moustache down the loo in triumphant celebration. I was not to know that the RSC was going to America at the end of the Stratford season, taking two plays, one of which required me, yet again, to suffer the spirit gum and surgical spirit torture combo.

With the onset of middle age, I was delighted to discover that some weird hormonal change now made it possible for me to grow my own moustache and beard. Trouble is, now I don't have enough hormonal energy to support the hair on my head. I guess you win some, you lose some...

PS

When I told Peter Robertson, former Scoutmaster and a well-established Letham worthy, that with my brother Bill I was going to spend a night on a fishing boat going to the Bell Rock, off Arbroath, and that we had been advised to take sandwiches, Peter replied: "Tak' sardines. They're used tae the sea."

There's hardly been a week in my adult life when I have not sent up a silent prayer of gratitude to whichever deity is in charge of these things, for my extraordinary good fortune in being born at that time, into that family, into that community, into that country. Lucky, or what?

Printed in Dunstable, United Kingdom

68651095R00113